Readings in the Christian Initiation of Children

# Font and Table Series

The Font and Table Series offers pastoral perspectives on Christian baptism, confirmation and eucharist.

Other titles in the series are:

A Catechumenate Needs Everybody:
Study Guide for Parish Ministers

At that Time: Cycles and Seasons in the Life of a Christian

Baptism: A Parish Celebration

Baptism Is a Beginning

Celebrating the Rites of Adult Initiation: Pastoral Reflections

The Church Speaks about Sacraments with Children:
Baptism, Confirmation, Eucharist, Penance

Confirmation: A Parish Celebration

Confirmed as Children, Affirmed as Teens

Finding and Forming Sponsors and Godparents

Guide for Sponsors

How Does a Person Become a Catholic?

How to Form a Catechumenate Team

Infant Baptism: A Parish Celebration

Issues in the Christian Initiation of Children

Welcoming the New Catholic

When Should We Confirm? The Order of Initiation

Related and available through Liturgy Training Publications:

The Rite of Christian Initiation of Adults (ritual and study editions)

Rito de la Iniciación de Adultos (ritual and study editions)

Catechumenate: A Journal of Christian Initiation

Readings in the Christian Initiation of Children

VICTORIA M. TUFANO, EDITOR

Introduction by
James W. Moudry

Liturgy Training Publications

Acknowledgments

We are grateful to Jerry Pottebaum of Treehaus Publications, who first suggested that we undertake this project; to Gael Gensler and Ron Oakham, who at that time were on the staff of The North American Forum on the Catechumenate; to Thom Morris, the executive director of Forum, for suggesting articles; to Jim Moudry of the Institute for the Christian Initiation of Children, for his help in selecting and ordering these articles; to Dan Connors of Twenty-third Publications, for locating some of the articles; and to the owners of the copyrights of the various articles in this book, for their permission to reprint them.

All references to the *Rite of Christian Initiation of Adults* are based on the text and paragraph numbers of the 1988 edition: © 1985, International Committee on English in the Liturgy; © 1988, United States Catholic Conference.

"The Christian Initiation of Children" by Christiane Brusselmans first appeared in the newsletter of The North American Forum on the Catechumenate, Fall 1986. References to the *Rite of Christian Initiation of Adults* have been edited to reflect the 1988 edition. © 1986 by Christiane Brusselmans. Reprinted with permission.

"Catechumenate for Children: Sharing the Gift of Faith" by Catherine Dooley is taken from *The Living Light* © June 1988 by the United States Catholic Conference, Washington, D.C. 20017-1194 and is used with permission. All rights reserved.

"Unbaptized Children: A Parish Challenge" by Richelle Pearl-Koller first appeared in *Today's Parish,* March 1992. © 1992 by Richelle Pearl-Koller. Reprinted with permission.

"Unbaptized Children: What Can We Do?" by Don Neumann first appeared in two parts in *Today's Parish,* September and October, 1988. © 1988 by Don Neumann. Reprinted with permission.

"Statement on the Pastoral Challenge of Implementing the *Rite of Christian Initiation of Adults* for Children Who Have Reached Catechetical Age" is taken from the *Rite of Christian Initiation of Adults* © 1988 by the United States Catholic Conference, Washington, D.C. 20017-1194 and is used with permission. All rights reserved.

The following articles first appeared in *Catechumenate: A Journal of Christian Initiation:*

"Let the Children Come to Me" by James B. Dunning first appeared in two parts in September and November 1988; "The Rite of Christian Initiation Adapted for Children: First Steps" by Gael Gensler, May 1990;

"Christian Initiation of Children: Introduction to the Text" by Frank C. Sokol, November 1988; "Christian Initiation of Children: No Longer a Class or Grade Issue" by Steven M. Robich, January 1989; "Children, Scrutinies and Penitential Rites" by Richelle Pearl-Koller © March 1992, used with permission; "Confirmation: Sponsors, Godparents and Parents" by Robert D. Duggan, January 1991; "Prebaptismal and Postbaptismal Catechesis in Early Childhood" by Jeanette Lucinio, July 1989; "Caring for the Anawim: Catechetical Age Children" by Don Neumann, July 1988; "What Should We Ask of Child Catechumens?" by Rita Burns Senseman, September 1991.

"Children's Initiation: Are we ready?" by James B. Dunning, "How Did We Get Where We Are and Where Do We Go from Here?" by Frank C. Sokol and "A Parish Experience" by Richard P. Moudry were delivered at the first Consultation on the Catechumenate for Children, convened by The North American Forum on the Catechumenate, December 4–6, 1988. They were first published in *Catechumenate: A Journal of Christian Initiation,* March 1989.

Copyright © 1994, Archdiocese of Chicago: Liturgy Training Publications, 1800 North Hermitage Avenue, Chicago IL 60622-1101; 1-800-933-1800, FAX 1-800-933-7094. All rights reserved.
Production editor: Deborah Bogaert
Copy editing and permissions: Jennifer McGeary
Design: Kerry Perlmutter
Typesetting: Mark Hollopeter
Cover art by Sarah Perlmutter.
Photographs by Antonio Perez.
This book was set in Futura and Garamond.

Printed in the United States of America.

Library of Congress Cataloging-in-Publication Data

Readings in the Christian initiation of children/Victoria M. Tufano, editor; introduction by James W. Moudry.
    p. cm. — (Font and table series)
   Includes index.
    1. Catechetics — Catholic Church. 2. Christian education of children. 3. Initiation rites — Religious aspects — Catholic Church. 4. Catholic Church. Ordo initaitionis Christianae adultorum.
I. Tufano, Victoria M., 1952– . II. Series.
BX1968.R37 1994
264'.020812 — dc20   94-22214
                                                                                               CIP

Contents

Introduction
James W. Moudry   viii

Part One : **The Reform of the Initiation of Children**

Let the Children Come to Me: Christian Initiation of Children
James B. Dunning   4

Children's Initiation: Are we ready?
James B. Dunning   26

The Christian Initiation of Children
Christiane Brusselmans   34

A Parish Experience
Richard P. Moudry   44

Part Two: **Working with the Reformed Rite**

Christian Initiation of Children: Introduction to the Text
Frank C. Sokol   58

Catechumenate for Children: Sharing the Gift of Faith
Catherine Dooley   66

Unbaptized Children: A Parish Challenge
Richelle Pearl-Koller   84

Unbaptized Children: What Can We Do?
Don Neumann   92

**The Rite of Christian Initiation Adapted for Children:
First Steps**
Gael Gensler   104

**Christian Initiation of Children:
No Longer a Class or Grade Issue**
Steven M. Robich   110

Children, Scrutinies and Penitential Rites
Richelle Pearl-Koller   116

Confirmation: Sponsors, Godparents and Parents
Robert D. Duggan   124

Part Three: **Pastoral Issues in Implementing the Rite**

**Prebaptismal and Postbaptismal Catechesis
in Early Childhood**
Jeanette Lucinio   134

Caring for the Anawim: Catechetical Age Children
Don Neumann   144

What Should We Ask of Child Catechumens?
Rita Burns Senseman   152

**How Did We Get Where We Are
and Where Do We Go from Here?**
Frank C. Sokol   164

**Statement on the Pastoral Challenge of Implementing
the *Rite of Christian Initiation of Adults* for Children
Who Have Reached Catechetical Age**
Bishops' Committee on the Liturgy, Committee on Pastoral
Research and Practices, and Committee on Education   172

Authors   184

Introduction

When the *Ordo Initiationis Christianae Adultorum* was promulgated in 1972, its provision for the initiation of unbaptized children of catechetical age went virtually unnoticed. Neither did the appearance of the English *Rite of Christian Initiation of Adults* in 1974 draw much attention to the section on children. The reason, of course, was that the principal thrust of the document was toward the situation of unbaptized adults, and that is where pastoral energy focused. Furthermore, the use of the rite by parishes was allowed by the implementing decree of 1972, but it was not required. Thus for more than a decade, with some important exceptions, little attention was given to the rite's directives about unbaptized children of catechetical age.

The atmosphere changed in 1988 when the revised English edition was published in the United States and became mandatory on September 1 of that year. Parishes that had implemented the adult portion of the rite began to confront part II: "Rite for Particular Circumstances" and in particular, "The Christian Initiation of Children Who Have Reached Catechetical Age." They discovered, to their surprise, that frequently it was more difficult to implement the reform of initiation for children than for adults. Should that have come as a surprise? Not really. The implications of the reform of children's initiation reach deep into the life of a parish and challenge its customary ways of thinking about sacraments for children.

What pastoral ministers have discovered is that the "new way" of initiating adults in the parish met with little resistance (except for those few people who resent any lengthening of "their Mass" by the occasional celebration of the catechumenal rites on a Sunday). The reason is because very few Catholics had any idea of how adult "non-Catholics" came to be Catholic. Whatever happened to those converts happened in the privacy of the parish rectory and was "between Father and them." What most Catholics observed, if they noticed anything at all, was that this person, who used to remain in the pew, now was going to communion. So, they concluded, he or she must have been baptized and received into the church. How all that happened was a mystery. Most cared little about the process, since it did not affect them at all. Hence, when the church presented the new way for adults to become Christian, called "the RCIA" or "catechumenal ministry," most Catholics accepted it easily. After all, they had no personal investment in the old way.

But when it came to initiating children, the matter was quite different. Catholics know about children and what goes on in their religious formation. They know about infant baptism, about first confession and first communion around age seven, and they know about confirmation at age ten or twelve (or, more recently, at age sixteen or seventeen). And Catholic parents know about religious education programs, Catholic parish schools, CCD classes and catechisms. They know all about these realities from guiding their own children through those years and from personal memories of their own experience of childhood sacraments. Hence, when the church presents the new way of making Catholic Christians out of unbaptized seven-year-old children, most Catholic laity have a point of reference from which to respond and critique the new practice.

One may object that the new practice really ought not to draw much attention because, after all, there are not that many unbaptized seven-year-olds in most parishes. That is true. But those children who do fit into the category addressed by the rite also fit into groupings of the other children of the parish. There are both baptized and unbaptized children of "catechetical age" in the same classrooms, sometimes in the same families. But the church's response to each is different, sometimes wildly different, which, of course, raises questions among parents and children. Why is it that the unbaptized schoolmate, brother or sister can "become Catholic by getting all three sacraments (baptism, confirmation and eucharist) together," while "my child has to wait and do so many more things because those sacraments are separated"? There are countless variations on the theme.

What the above scenario points to is the potential impact of the reform of children's initiation ministry on existing programs of catechesis and sacramental preparation. Let me name but two. The rite's requirement to initiate the unbaptized children with the full celebration of three initiation sacraments, preferably at the Easter Vigil with adult candidates, forces the question of the proper sequence of the sacraments of baptism, confirmation and first eucharist. Specifically, it raises the question of the proper placement (not age, which is the wrong question) of the sacrament of confirmation. Some parishes have begun to take the first step toward bringing parish patterns of children's sacraments into harmony with the reform by celebrating the sacrament of confirmation at the Mass marking the child's first reception of the eucharist. In the experience of one parish (see the article by Richard Moudry in this volume), it was only when the parish restored the sequence of the sacraments for their baptized Catholic children that the vision of the *Rite of Christian Initiation of Adults* began to penetrate the parish at large. The vision in question has to do with fostering the paschal quality of Christian spirituality and ecclesial piety which are, arguably, the principal goal of the entire liturgical renewal in the Catholic church in this century.

The second challenge of the reform to existing practice is in the area of catechesis. "The message to the People of God" of the Synod of Bishops on *Catechesis in Our Time* in 1977 calls the catechumenate "the model" for all catechesis, and the National Catechetical Directory, *Sharing the Light of Faith,* states that the catechumenate provides a norm for all catechetical as well as liturgical practice with regard to initiation (#115; references found in Catherine Dooley's article in this volume). The catechesis of the catechumenate is frankly liturgical (cf. RCIA, 75). It is a catechesis that locates the liturgical experience at the heart of the catechetical effort, where it functions as the source of faith reflection and Christian action. Catechumenal catechesis regards the child's liturgical experience as the centerpiece of religious and spiritual formation, not as an afterthought.

The current trend toward "lectionary-based catechesis" is an effort in the direction of making catechesis relate more organically to liturgy. Thus far, the results have been quite uneven, principally because the effort has been more about lectionary than about liturgy. The value of a properly done, separate celebration of the liturgy of the word with children (described in the *Directory for Masses with Children,* 17) is that it provides children with a liturgical experience of God's word (including a "homiletic reflection") which subsequently — after the liturgy — serves as the basis of faith exploration with the help of a knowledgeable catechist. This was the insight of the late Christiane Brusselmans. She saw separate celebrations of the liturgy of the word for children as a key building block for the Christian initiation of children, both the unbaptized child and the Catholic child baptized in infancy, who is completing her/his sacramental initiation. Finding the way toward the catechetical style of the catechumenate is a major challenge to those who traditionally have been charged with the responsibility for guiding children through the initiation experience.

I have mentioned two challenges that flow from the implementation of the reformed rites of initiation. There are others. It should not be thought, in any case, that the section of the RCIA applying to unbaptized children is a perfect document. Far from it. The review of the children's initiation rites currently being undertaken by the International Committee on English in the Liturgy (ICEL) is welcome. Pastoral use of the document has shown that both clarification and revision are needed. For example, who exactly is the "peer group" (RCIA, 254), and does the document intend to recognize among children the existence of a "candidate" comparable to the adult "candidate"? What does conversion mean in the case of a young child? What is the sacrament of penance doing in the midst of a scrutiny? Why does the scrutiny for children become so anemic? There is also a need to find liturgical language more suited to the situation of children. But all of those adjustments, should they be made, will be fine-tuning. The basic pattern of the reform with its underlying principles is set for the initiation of both adults and children. And it is that pattern and vision, particularly as they apply to children, which are a delight, hope and challenge to our way of being church.

The first task to be accomplished, however, is to support the efforts of parishes to develop a strong initiation ministry with children. This volume hopes to encourage a thoughtful implementation of the rite. Collected here are articles on children's initiation published over the past few years, which heretofore have not been collected into a single volume. As such this book stands as a companion to other collections from Liturgy Training Publications: *Issues in the Christian Initiation of Children: Catechesis and Liturgy*, edited by Kathy Brown and Frank Sokol (1989); *When Should We Confirm?* (1989) and *Confirmed as Children, Affirmed As Teens: The Order of Initiation* (1990), both edited by James Wilde.

Part one of this book deals with the vision, the over-arching principles and the structural ramifications of the reform of Christian initiation given to us in the *Rite of Christian Initiation of Adults*. Jim Dunning starts off by locating our practices of initiation within a larger historical picture, illuminating thereby some of our present pastoral inconsistencies. He then situates the initiation of children within the context of adult initiation and offers models of how we might organize the former. In a subsequent article, he turns around the customary question, "Are the children ready for sacraments?" to ask "Are we (the community and family) ready to undertake the initiating ministry?" By posing the question in this way, Dunning de-privatizes initiation and gives it an ecclesial footing.

The late Christiane Brusselmans gives her inimitable views on the sacramental patterns of children's initiation from the perspective of her rich personal and pastoral experiences. Richard Moudry concludes part one by describing how the parish he served as pastor began to catch the vision of initiation when they restored the sacraments to the sequence set forth in the RCIA and in other church reform documents.

Part two gathers articles that explore the workings of the rite. The late Frank Sokol takes us step by step through the all-important introductory paragraphs of the section on children's initiation. Catherine Dooley follows with a penetrating overview of the rite itself. She identifies and critiques the inconsistencies that prove so vexing when trying to implement the rite. She concludes with a series of implications and challenges.

Richelle Pearl-Koller describes how important it is for catechumenal ministers to adopt the proper attitude in approaching the rite. We need a new mind-set. In a similar vein, Don Neumann's article shows how the new rite can change our entire approach to the initiation of children. He raises tough questions about the reform of initiation practices with children and concludes by suggesting a model for how to work with the rite in a new pastoral setting.

Gael Gensler reminds us that the adult rite serves as the context for understanding and implementing the section on children. The late Steven Robich invites us into the conversation about the new shape of catechesis called for by the rite, a conversation, as noted above, that remains very lively. Richelle Pearl-Koller returns to scrutinize the scrutinies as they appear in the children's adaptation and poses some penetrating questions. Why does the meaning of a scrutiny get watered down for children? Why is the ritual confused by introducing the possibility of a first celebration of penance for the baptized companions? And finally, in a helpful, short article, Robert Duggan clarifies the question of sponsors for confirmation and, in so doing, illumines again the intimate relationship between baptism and confirmation.

In part three the reader will find articles that deal with some of the particular aspects of implementation. Jeanette Lucinio reminds us that the child's spiritual life thrives on ritual. She shows how catechesis, especially with young children, needs to build on that experience. Don Neumann makes a pastoral plea for nonjudgmental acceptance of Catholic parents who bring older children for baptismal initiation. He sees this as a test of the community's commitment to the gospel values of hospitality and reconciliation. Rita Burns Senseman poses the question, "What should we ask of child catechumens," particularly as that relates to their conversion. Conversion requirements must be age appropriate, and conversion itself needs to become manifest in life behavior and not just in mind. She cites examples from the life experience of teenagers. Frank Sokol recalls the principal factors in the twentieth-century catechetical movement and their implications for the reform of children's initiation. He points out directions for the future.

Finally, there is the U.S. bishops' committees' "Statement on the Pastoral Challenge of Implementing the *Rite of Christian Initiation of Adults* for Children" (1990). The bishops acknowledge the complexity of the current pastoral situation:

> Thus, within the same family, individuals may be initiated at different times and in different ways, depending on their age, whether or not they have been baptized and the extent to which they have been previously formed in the Christian life.

That analysis should bring comfort to pastoral ministers. The subsequent statement may not:

> Those responsible for catechesis must clearly explain to families the various approaches to the Christian formation and sacramental initiation of their family members that correspond to these different factors.

Many ministers would wish that the church could come to a consistent policy regarding children's initiation. It would make their catechetical responsibilities easier. Perhaps in wrestling with the challenges presented by the rite, greater clarity and firmer purpose will emerge regarding a consistent initiatory policy for children. Let us hope so.

Liturgy Training Publications deserves our thanks for their willingness to assemble these articles into a book of readings. The ministry of Christian initiation of children is still in its beginning stage. We can benefit from hearing the wisdom, experience and insights of our colleagues in this ministry. Equally as important, we can be inspired by their obvious love for and commitment to the children. Jesus said that the reign of God belongs to the children. Like him, we will do well to stand the child in our midst and let the child show us the way.

James W. Moudry
Institute for the Christian Initiation of Children

PART ONE:

The Reform of the Initiation of Children

Let the Children Come to Me: Christian Initiation of Children

JAMES B. DUNNING

That shy person of the airwaves, Garrison Keillor, describes sacramental life at Lake Wobegon's Catholic church, Our Lady of Perpetual Responsibility.

> [I was] tainted with a sneaking admiration of Catholics—Catholic Christmas, Easter, the Living Rosary, and the Blessing of the Animals, all magnificent . . . especially the Feast Day of St. Francis, which they did right out in the open, a feast for the eyes. Cows, horses, some pigs, right on the church lawn. The turmoil, animals bellowing and barking and clucking . . . and the ocarina band of third graders playing Catholic dirges, and the great calm of the sisters, and the flags and the Knights of Columbus decked out in their handsome black suits—I stared at it until my eyes almost fell out. . . . I wasn't allowed inside the church, of course, but if the Blessing of the Animals on the Feast Day of St. Francis was any indication, Lord, I didn't know but what they had elephants in there and acrobats.[1]

If Garrison loves that feast day, he will salivate over the galaxy of rites and symbols, vesture and gesture, smells and bells of the *Rite of Christian Initiation of Adults* (RCIA) with its welcomes, processions, signings, blessings, exorcisms, calling of names, signing of books, scrutinizing, laying on of hands, immersing, anointing, eating, drinking, replete with the Book of the Elect, water, white garments, candles, oil, bread and wine, and the great sacrament of Christ's presence—an assembly called church, truly a "feast for the eyes." Belloc's little ditty is enfleshed in the RCIA: "Where e'er the Catholic sun doth shine, there's music and laughter and good red wine. At least I've heard them tell it so, *benedicamus Domino!*"

We will explore implications of the adult rite for the initiation of children, but first some disclaimers. Number one: I rarely minister with children. I am one of the church's great plagiarizers, so I shall steal from those who do.

Second, since adult initiation for the unbaptized involves baptism, confirmation and eucharist, in that order and at one celebration, that raises enormous questions for the practice with children of baptism, reconciliation, eucharist and confirmation in that order, spread over several years. I cannot possibly deal with all the approaches to this, especially to confirmation. For the latter, please consult three articles in *PACE* 17 (Winona MN: St. Mary's Press, 1986–87), which has more theories than the Spirit has gifts. I shall explore one approach: restoring to children the order celebrated with adults. Most agree that the vast weight of historical and theological evidence supports that approach. I suggest that it also makes more sense pastorally because confirmation as puberty rite or maturity rite for many youth becomes not a rite of commitment but of exit.

Third, under present canon law and practice, some options are impossible today. They are like the series called *Alternative Futures for Worship* (Collegeville: The Liturgical Press, 1987), which describes rites for tomorrow which we cannot celebrate today. We may need 25 years of experience with the order of Christian initiation before they are possible. But much in the *Rite of Christian Initiation of Adults* can inform and reform our ministry with children so that what we do today opens possibilities for tomorrow.

What I shall do is: 1) survey the history; 2) review some results of that history; 3) situate rites of initiation where all sacraments have their roots: in Jesus and church as sacraments; 4) explore adult initiation as the normative rite; 5) offer models of what can be done today and what might be done tomorrow.

HISTORY: THE WAY WE AREN'T

The early tradition of the West and also the unchanging tradition of the East (Catholic and Orthodox) is that baptism-confirmation-eucharist is the rite of initiation for infants and adults. The *Rite of Christian Initiation of Adults* restores that for adults. In those early years, St. Cyprian insisted that the eucharistic assembly *is* the church. Members (including infants) become members through rites, including eucharist.[2] Aidan Kavanagh claims that the two great sacraments were baptism (including an anointing) and eucharist; confirmation was most likely a minor rite in which the bishop dismissed the newly baptized from the baptistry to the church for eucharist.[3] In the East until today and "in the early Christian West, baptism and eucharist were inseparable, to the extent that baptism without eucharist is not initiation into the church. . . . Initiation into the Christian community was not dependent on the rational capabilities of the recipient. . . . The model idealized the pre-rational. The newly baptized were inwardly infants (regardless of age) and were given the food for infants."[4]

In the West the dissolution of the rites of initiation began with the separation of confirmation, not for theological reasons but by accident: the decreasing number and unavailability of bishops. Bishops inveighed against delaying confirmation, but they reserved it to themselves and it became more distant from baptism. Eucharist remained connected to baptism in some regions until the Council of Trent, especially wine for infants. In most areas, however, the barring of laity from the cup and the theology of transubstantiation with its rationalistic theory of real presence had separated eucharist from baptism by the twelfth century. Also in that same century, because of over-emphasis on Christ's divinity and our unworthiness to receive him, the church legislated that adults receive eucharist once a year. The eucharist was effectively denied to infants. By the Council of Trent in the seventeenth century, the three sacraments of initiation were "left to flounder without a structure to provide a sense of continuity and meaning. This not only threatened the initiatory identity of each sacrament, it also left each sacrament bereft of any appropriate catechetical and pastoral practices pertaining to their reception."[5]

After Trent we filled that void with catechesis of infants by parents, catechesis by the school for penance followed by confirmation, and catechesis for first eucharist at around ages 12 to 14. At least the order was somewhat restored. In 1910 Pope Pius X upended that catechesis by issuing *Quam Singulari*. He sought to undo abuses of Jansenism by lowering the age for first eucharist to about the age of seven, which gave catechists the dilemma of preparing children for penance, confirmation and eucharist at the same time.

That broke our catechetical backs. Confirmation moved its way up into the eighth grade and now into adolescence, although canon 891 of the revised code of canon law puts confirmation at the age of reason, a law circumvented in the United States. Some claim it is not traditional to put confirmation before eucharist. They turned a 70-year-old custom into a tradition! We also have bishops who complain about all these confirmations but really love to flee their desks and minister to youth.

DISASTROUS RESULTS

What are the results? First, we made a minor rite into a big deal. We devalued our two great sacraments, baptism and eucharist. Any priest can baptize. It takes a bishop to confirm! Baptism and eucharist summon everyone to mission. Sometimes delayed confirmation implied we were out there on the front lines without the Spirit.

Second, confirmation with adolescents "puts the gift of the Spirit in a context which inevitably interprets the sacrament less in terms of a transforming conversion and initiation into eucharistic and ecclesial fellowship than of education and solving adolescent personality problems consequent upon puberty and entry into civil society."[6] For practical reasons youth minister John Roberto insists this is the wrong time for many youth. Some see it as one more hoop coercing them into religion class, through which they have to jump and after which they drop out.

> This coercion may be one factor which leads many young people to regard confirmation as the special event which marks their "graduation" from ecclesiastical constraint into the apparent freedoms of secular life. While education and therapy doubtless need to be done, these endeavors must not be allowed to reinterpret sacraments . . . to the extent that sacraments and liturgy become unintelligible apart from such educational and therapeutic endeavors.[7]

Third, French catechist Didier Piviteau argues we are asking too much of the school. Christian cultures initiated children into conversion and church by osmosis, with stories of faith passed on by family, neighborhood, holy days and the entire culture. The school offered reflection on faith already present. In clearly secularized France and less clearly secularized America, when people claim belief in God but their families collapse, their gods become mammon and power. When a chief purveyor of the stories in America are soaps—with their version of "Another World," "Days of our Lives" and "One Life to Live"—classes and catechisms don't make it. Piviteau says we knew that. Therefore, we made catechetics less cognitive, more existential. "The church has developed tremendously the schooling approach to Religious Education (formal catechetics) but has used the structure to try to foster initiation, a task for which it has never been meant."[8]

Piviteau contrasts initiation with schooling. Initiation "functions like a matrix giving birth not to a carnal body but to a corporate mind and heart." Society must be stable and unanimous. The process is not limited to specific times, places or educators. It transmits not just knowledge but stories, traditions, behaviors and values that cement a community. It is not just for primitive tribes; it is still how infants learn a language. Schooling is specialized, happens in specific hours and days, with teachers. It transmits facts, concepts, laws, theories and critical attitudes. Piviteau concludes our urgent task is to build new forms of church since initiating communities have collapsed and schools are failing as substitutes. That means we have to find what type of community is valid today.[9]

Fourth and most telling, in our eucharist we ignore the words of the Lord. The story of Jesus blessing children is in all three synoptics. After the disciples scolded people for bringing children, Jesus retorts, "Let the children come to me, and do not hinder them, because the reign of God belongs to such as these" (Mark 10:14; cf. Matthew 19:13–14; Luke 18:15–16). He says, unless we become like children we shall not enter that realm. He rejoices that what God hides from the wise he reveals to babes (cf. Matthew 11:26; Luke 10:21). He sets a child in their midst as an example (Matthew 18:2–3; Luke 9:47–48). He says God's glory is sung through the mouths of babes (Matthew 21:16). He calls his disciples "children" (cf. John 21:15). Jesus puts infants at center stage; the church keeps them in the vestibule. We are disciples who scold and hinder children. An Orthodox priest remarks that for Paul there was neither Jew nor gentile, slave nor free, male nor female. For the church there are adults and children.[10]

The road to that division is cluttered with debris. First, we misinterpret 1 Corinthians 11:27–28, where Paul charged that those who eat and drink "without discerning the body" drink judgment upon themselves. We made a catechetical enterprise of teaching cognitively that Jesus is in bread and wine, while Paul talked about community. We are judged if we do not see Christ in that body. That is precisely what we do with children when we deny that they are the body and refuse to welcome them in communion.

Second, rationalism infects our religious education. John Sutcliffe researched children in 30 countries. He found their order of experience: "First, through birth and baptism they belong to Christ. Second, they experience that they belong and grow to believe it to be so. And third, they acknowledge and profess and, maybe, understand their belonging."[11] We withhold eucharist from children on the grounds that they can't understand, which is as absurd as withholding affection because they don't understand. Such a standard would exclude the confused elderly and the mentally disabled.

Even adults in the early church received catechesis about eucharist during mystagogy *after* initiation at the Easter Vigil. We sometimes reduce catechesis to cognitive content. That is a concern in days of "the closing of the American (and religious) mind." But the early church knew that we *learn* sacraments by *experiencing* sacraments. We *become* the body of Christ by *being* the body of Christ. Knowledge without experience can be Paul's noisy gongs and clanging bells. But if psychologists insist on the importance of infants' experience, if sociologists value the dynamic impact of early socialization, if catechetical theorists see that there is not only cognitive content but affective content, nonverbal, unconscious and lifestyle content,[12] then at an early age we welcome children to smells and bells, gesture and vesture, water, oil, bread and wine, that "feast for the eyes" which made Garrison Keillor's eyes almost fall out. That assumes, of course, that catechesis happens with grand Catholic largesse and splendor with robust symbols. It assumes baptism by immersion (who ever got sprinkled to death?), lots of oil (little dabs will not "do ya"), and bread and wine that are really a meal (some claim it's harder to believe a wafer is bread than to believe that it's the body of Christ).

Third, a privatized view of eucharist does not "discern the body," does not see eucharist as belonging in a community. It delays eucharist until children understand it as a union of "Jesus and me." After research with children, David Holeton came to this hypothesis:

> The practice of the communion of young children and infants varies directly with the sense of community within the church. . . . Where the church sees itself as a community that takes seriously the importance of the individual in the corporate whole, then infants and young children will receive the eucharist.[13]

Exclusion from eucharist drew these responses from children: "You say Jesus asks us to come to his table, so why do you stop us?" "I'm not going to say, 'We are all one body' again, because we aren't. Me and Ben don't share the bread." One four-year-old wished he could take communion because "I belong to the church, you know."[14] A mother writes, "Melinda, age 4, after receiving communion felt that Jesus Christ was part of her. She did not understand how." Belonging to the body of Christ is not primarily cognitive. Who knows what we communicate to children when they are warmly welcomed into communion with the body of Christ by the body of Christ? We often see babies reach out for the bread, perhaps intuitively knowing: To eat with the community is to be the community. Some offer a blessing as an alternative; but while eating seems clear to children, blessings may not be. One child remarked that he just had his head measured.

JESUS AND CHURCH AS SACRAMENTS

If Holeton is right that we welcome these children to the extent that we see church as community, what is the relationship of that community to us and to the Christ of God? Much post-Vatican theology proclaims Christ is *the* sacrament of God, and the church is *the* sacrament of Christ. John Shea writes: "The code word 'incarnation' is the central affirmation of Christian faith. It says that God's commitment to the human adventure is not a word of promise from a distant reality but a personal union with a human life."[15] Catholics and other sacramental churches take incarnation with radical seriousness. The Word becomes flesh in Jesus; he is the "primordial sacrament" of God's presence in our world. "When one says baptism, the first thought one should have is 'Jesus,' not water, original sin, or entrance into the church."[16] The church is the "basic sacrament." The seven derivative sacraments and the 70 times 7 sacramentals at Our Lady of Perpetual Responsibility are not things but actions of Christ through that basic sacrament: the church initiating into community, eating and drinking in communion, reconciling, healing, leading, marrying.

Buckminster Fuller said, "For me God is more verb than noun." That holds for sacraments. They are actions we do to be church.[17]

Transubstantiation focused on real presence in bread and wine (often seen as objects—not actions—of a shared thanksgiving meal). Eucharist often became just things, reified, "thingified." Priests were the ones "in on the action." The basic sacrament became a privatized automat. Juan Segundo writes: "The eucharist brings people next to each other; it juxtaposes them. It doesn't make a community out of participants."[18]

In its most explosive paragraph, the *Constitution on the Sacred Liturgy* expands Christ's real presence to: word, ministries, ritual action with bread and wine, and, most important, the community (cf. #7).[19] The purpose of this real presence in word, ministries and the ritual action of all seven sacraments is to express and deepen the presence in a community. Why is it, then, that we remain juxtaposed? Why do we kneel before the bread and kill each other in the parking lot? I once extended my hand for the exchange of peace and got back a printed card which read, "We shouldn't be shaking hands. We should be praying to Jesus!"

IMPLICATIONS OF THE *RITE OF CHRISTIAN INITIATION OF ADULTS* FOR THE INITIATION OF CHILDREN

Into that privatized scene enters the *Rite of Christian Initiation of Adults* with a key paragraph:

> The initiation of catechumens is a gradual process that takes place within the community of the faithful. By joining the catechumens in reflecting on the value of the paschal mystery and by renewing their own conversion, the faithful provide an example that will help the catechumens to obey the Holy Spirit more generously. (#4)

That paragraph sets the norm for all initiation.

When Aidan Kavanagh stirred up the baptismal waters by saying precisely that adult initiation is the norm, there were howls of protest. People thought he was throwing babies out with the bath water. No way. We live after Freud; we see the critical need to initiate infants in a community of love. We reshaped our theology; we see original sin not as a black mark inflicted by our first parents but as systems of sin built by all parents and adults that bombard infants from day one. We need a community to bombard infants with grace from day one.

Adult initiation as the norm, however, means we do with children what we do with adults. How does the basic sacrament, the church, act in the order of initiation? What does that imply for our actions with children?

We Journey in Community First, we journey. Initiation for adults is neither a magic moment of pouring water nor a terminal program of six weeks,[20] but a galaxy of rites which are *part of the sacrament,* the community acting in myriad ways. The very first time the community acts publicly in the rite of acceptance into the order of catechumens, the presider says, "Joined to the church, the catechumens are now part of the household of Christ" (RCIA, 471). They are apprentice members living in a community of grace *before baptism.* Many sacramental programs for parents of infants to be baptized end with baptism. Yet adults journey after baptism for 50 days of mystagogy, a year of at least monthly sessions and a lifetime of ongoing conversion.

Second, we journey in community. The process of initiation is less an inquiry class than an AA group of peers and sponsors, all of whom have wisdom because they've "been there." Joined to Christ in the Spirit, all of this community has "been there": catechumens, evangelizers, ministers of hospitality, sponsors, catechists, presbyters, spiritual directors, musicians, liturgists, deacons, mystagogues, presiders, parish council members, bishops, the liturgical assembly—the body of Christ. We *enter* the body of Christ by *meeting* the body of Christ.

Implications for Initiating Infants. First, we support parents and families at sessions before and after initiation. Second, those sessions address the real needs of families. We ask questions like, "What are your hopes and fears for your children?" and "How is communication in your marriage?" not just "What is the meaning of water?" Third, those sessions are largely led by peers who have "been there." Fourth, if godparents who are relatives are unable to be part of the process, we give the family parish sponsors. Fifth, in most cases we shall continue to initiate infants. Church policy is that we cannot deny baptism; we can delay it until parents show signs they will support their child in faith. Then, we don't turn them away.

We meet with parents and children to help them grow in faith. Growth in faith is not just Mass attendance. We often need to meet with grandparents who may exert pressure because of the specter of limbo. If time-scarred adults are joined to Christ before baptism, we can certainly hope newborn babes are in God's hands. Fifth, the church treats older children (from the age of reason) as adults. Strictly speaking, there is no "RCIC"; there are adapted rites for children in part II of the RCIA.

We Proclaim the Word (Evangelize and Catechize) and We Throw Parties (Celebrate Liturgies).

We proclaim the word. The goal of evangelization that takes place in the period of inquiry is "faith and initial conversion that cause a person to feel called away from sin and drawn into the mystery of God's love" (RCIA, 36–37).

The goal of the second period, the catechumenate, is deepening faith by breaking open the scriptures of the lectionary, entering the community life of prayer and moral values, celebrating rites and witnessing actively to faith, especially for justice (RCIA, 75). The order of initiation assumes that catechumens in a Spirit-filled community come not just for information, doctrine and knowledge about God but for a personal relationship with God. This confronts Jim Fowler's research that many people believe with group—not personal—faith, Gallup's research that Catholics scored lowest in agreeing with the statement that "God loves you a great deal" (65 percent) and in believing they have a personal relationship with God (82 percent), and Hoge's research that 38 percent of all priests and

55 percent of those 55 to 65 years old say faith is "belief in the doctrines of the Catholic church."[21]

We use the lectionary to proclaim that word. Like an Indianapolis parish that provides resources for all parish groups to gather 'round those readings, like a homily planning team, like the Episcopal diocese of Colorado that provides materials for preschool through adult, we nourish people through what has been our most traditional catechesis: the Sunday readings.[22] As one preschool catechist said, "We give them scripture, scripture and more scripture."

We also throw parties, a galaxy of rites, all of which celebrate the conversions happening through hearing the word. The *Rite of Christian Initiation of Adults* weds catechesis and liturgy. Catechesis aims at transformation, not just information. It is more like a homily than a lecture. All catechesis flows into and flows from the rites. It is ritual catechesis.

Implications for Children. First, initiation of infants focuses on God's free gift of love, not our response in faith; on God's action, not the infant's. But all sacraments are for the church, not just the individual. Catechumens challenge the faith of the parish, especially through the parish's witness at the rites. Children challenge parents and parish to be a community of faith, one that is welcoming, healing, accepting and graciously loving in a world of unbelief, division, hurt, rejection, competition, violence and sin.

> Initiation is not merely something parents do for their children but something children also do for their parents. It is not something the parish does for the family but also something the family does for the parish. . . . Conversion and commitments are in order from the time the child is on the way.[23]

So if we assume some parents and parishioners are among those weak in personal faith, we offer not classes but proclamations of the word, evangelization for them.

Second, we also throw parties for children. Yes, if we truly proclaim that word and summon parishioners to commitment as a community, even those who watch their watches during infant initiation may become church. We don't do it every Sunday but at appropriate times, like Eastertime, All Saints Day, the Baptism of the Lord. With older children we celebrate the childrens' rites in the *Rite of Christian Initiation of Adults.*

We Die and Rise. The initiation journey is into the paschal mystery, dying and rising in Christ (cf. RCIA, 4, 81). In the early church when so many Christians were dying as martyrs, the church was countercultural. Instructions weren't enough for initiation. People needed strong personal faith plus the support of a community that shared that faith.

Implications for Children and Families. We need to translate the jargon of the paschal mystery into events in the lives of families. If sacraments are not things or empty rituals but actions of people who die and rise today and who bring that to eucharist, where do families die and rise?

They die when marriages die. They go on dying with lack of support for single-parent families. They die when parents feel so alone, when few seem to share their values and faith. They die in ways that everyone dies: addiction, unemployment, illness in the family, emotional and physical violence, cutthroat competition. Even loving is dying—to self and the "me generation," in sacrifice for baby and beloved. *Amore* in Italian has roots in *morte*—death. For infant initiation, some suggest that the image "born again" might be better than "dying and rising."

Sam Keen says that the baby's journey from womb to world is an image for a lifetime of birthpains. He writes:

> In the empty place between mother and child . . . when the umbilical cord is cut, a new being is created. Birth teaches us that we are alone. It imprints us with the fear that we may be abandoned and the hope that we may be reunited with the ground of our being. Love and knowledge are born where we least expect them, in the manger of nothingness, in the empty and anxious space that separates us from our [womb]. Every crisis in which the psyche is stretched, pushed and impelled

into a large world . . . will be symbolized by the trauma and triumph of birth. Without being born again, and again, there is no journey, no spirit, no love.[24]

How can both family (the domestic church) and parish offer a womb community in which birthpains and death give way to birth and life? If the family is dying in any way, can we offer life? If parents feel like catechumens in the Roman Empire, alone in their faith and values, can we offer small communities who share their dream? In a pluralistic world of competing values, families cannot go it alone. All the energy we give to children's programs may be for naught if children cannot see our values, the ways of our people, our common story lived as adults.[25]

Can we also celebrate the gifts a child brings: "a gift of new life because the energies of the newly born invigorate human community, . . . a gift of hope that reaffirms our belief in the future that God continues to make new . . . a gift of love because the spontaneous affection of an infant reminds us that transcending love is never conditional"?[26]

We Bathe, Anoint, Eat and Drink — in that Order. Canon law and the *Rite of Christian Initiation of Adults* restored baptism/confirmation/eucharist as the sacrament of initiation for adults. Aidan Kavanagh asserts that the reformed *Rite of Confirmation* of 1971 abolished "confirmation in all but name, turning it into a postbaptismal chrismation . . . de-emphasizing both the hand laying and exclusively episcopal ministry" and insisting that it lead into the eucharist.[27]

Implications for Children. Mark Searle says we have three choices. 1. Put confirmation where it came from, between baptism and eucharist, a minor rite best celebrated at Eastertime. 2. Accept that it developed an identity of its own in the Roman rite (but neither in the East nor in non-Roman Western churches, at least as a sacrament) and celebrate it as a step toward full initiation in eucharist. 3. Maintain it as a rite of mature commitment completing childhood catechesis. He discounts the third option for two reasons. "First, it has no basis in our Catholic tradition; and second, it subordinates the sacramental nature of confirmation to exploit its pedagogical usefulness."[28]

He prefers the first option and insists that if we want to take the second, i.e., to separate confirmation from baptism but celebrate it before first eucharist, we must answer two questions: "First, what are the ecclesial effects of confirmation—what practical difference does it make? Second, how are we to give practical expression to those effects? What will the confirmed be permitted to do or to be that is not permitted to the unconfirmed, and how will the church be the better for it?"[29] In practice, however, that might still say to people that baptism is just forgiveness of original sin (85 percent of Catholics in one survey said that that is its purpose) and that the Spirit doesn't arrive until confirmation.[30]

That is an assault on Catholic views about the dignity of baptism and our universal call to mission. Should one "cite the need for catechesis in preparation for receiving the Holy Spirit in confirmation, someone else might then ask why such catechesis is not therefore even more necessary for baptism. Unless one delays baptism it seems that the catechetical answer loses force. This delay is not in sight."[31]

Models for the Initiation of Children. What are the options? First, some assumptions. We need to take time. If we delay baptism, if we restore the order of baptism/confirmation/eucharist, if we welcome infants to eucharist, we need to remember that we have taught people well about limbo, confirmation as commitment and eucharist as "discerning the body" rationally in bread and wine. It takes time to restore a more genuinely Catholic tradition. When a certain bishop moved confirmation from eighth grade to high school, the friendly sons of St. Patrick disinvited him from their annual dinner. People may need to experience adult initiation before they see implications for children.

I offer three models. The first is followed by some parishes today; the other two are dreams.

Model 1	Model 2	Model 3
■ Infant baptism ■ Reconciliation offered ■ Confirmation with eucharist at age of reason ■ Lent/Easter rites	■ Infant baptism, confirmation and eucharist ■ Reconciliation ■ Lent/Easter rites	■ Child's catechumenate ■ Baptism, confirmation and eucharist at age of reason ■ Reconciliation ■ Lent/Easter Rites

The first model respects the order of the sacraments as well as infant baptism. Following canon law, we offer—not force—reconciliation before eucharist. Since confirmation/eucharist is separated from baptism, we need catechesis about the Spirit and chrismation at baptism.

The second model respects infant initiation, unifies the sacraments and moves away from a rationalistic denial of eucharist to infants (children are welcomed but not forced).

The third model might serve parents who need something like a children's catechumenate. We could celebrate a rite of acceptance with them and their child and give them a catechumenal community of faith and support. We assume the latter in all three models as well as confirming initiation through reconciliation and Lent/Easter.

CONCLUSION

I close with thoughts of how children might minister to us. If children are more active in our rites, if we give them the kind of respect that Maria Montessori did when she named her schools *Casa del Bambini,* "Children's House," if we gather families and households to support them with something like a catechumenate, if those households bring deeper faith to the *oikos,* the household of the church, might we become what Jesus told us to become: more like little children?

Augustine was fascinated with the sucking child as an image of the human condition, one of total helplessness. Might we learn from infants that at times we come to God helpless, not earning communion but gifted by God's love? Might our stale, ordered, rationalistic, cerebral liturgies be enlivened by childlike wonder, disorder, the nonrational, heart and hands as well as head? Might we become what Francis Thompson wrote of Shelley?

> Know you what it is to be a child?
> It is to be something very different from the man of today.
> It is to have a spirit yet streaming from the waters
>   of baptism;
>   it is to believe in love;
>   to believe in loveliness;
>   to believe in belief;
> It is to be so little that the elves can reach to whisper
>   in your ear;
> It is to turn pumpkins into coaches,
>   and mice into horses,
>   lowness into loftiness,
>   and nothing into everything.

No wonder Jesus commanded, "Let the children come to me. Of such is the reign of God."

Endnotes

1. Garrison Keillor, *Lake Wobegon Days* (New York: Penguin Books, 1986), 19.

2. Cf. Cyrille Argenti, "Children and the Eucharist," in *And Do Not Hinder Them,* Geiko Müller-Fahrenholz, editor (Geneva: World Council of Churches, 1982), 59–60.

3. Aidan Kavanagh, *Confirmation: Origins and Reform* (New York: Pueblo, 1988).

4. Argenti, op. cit., 62.

5. Linda Gaupin, "Confirmation, First Eucharist and Sacramental Order," *Assembly* 14:1 (September 1987), 380–82.

6. Kavanagh, op. cit., 109.

7. Ibid., 110.

8. Didier Piviteau, "School, Society and Catechetics," *Religious Education and the Future,* Dermot Lane, editor (New York: Paulist Press), 25.

9. Ibid., 21–22, 27.

10. Argenti, op. cit., 50.

11. John Sutcliffe, "Children and Holy Communion," in Müller-Fahrenholz, op. cit., 35.

12. Cf. James Michael Lee, *The Content of Religious Instruction* (Birmingham: Religious Education Press, 1985).

13. David R. Holeton, "Communion of Infants and Young Children," in Müller-Fahrenholz, op. cit., 59.

14. Sutcliffe, op. cit., passim.

15. John Shea, *The Spirit Master* (Chicago: Thomas More Press, 1987), 63.

16. Kenan Osborne, *The Christian Sacraments of Initiation: Baptism, Confirmation, Eucharist* (New York: Paulist Press, 1987), 81.

17. Mark Searle comments on shifts in sacramental theology: "What began as a recovery of the ecclesial dimension of the sacraments quickly led to further shifts: from speaking of sacraments as 'means of grace' to speaking of them as encounters with Christ himself; from thinking of them primarily as acts of God to thinking of them mainly as celebrations of the faith community; from seeing sacraments as momentary incursions from another world to seeing them as manifestations of the graced character of all human life; from interpreting them as remedies for sin and weakness to seeing them as promoting growth in Christ," in "Infant Baptism Reconsidered," *Baptism and Confirmation, Alternative Futures for Worship 2* (Collegeville: Liturgical Press, 1987), 15.

18. Juan Segundo, *The Sacraments Today* (Maryknoll, NY: Orbis, 1974), 10.

19. Kenan Osborne insists that the key to understanding sacraments is to recover this vision of Jesus and the community as sacraments: "Jesus is present, really present, in all the sacraments, not only in the eucharist, and it is the real presence of the Lord in the church and in each of the sacraments which is the constitutive relationship between the primordial sacramentality of the humanness of Jesus and all other derivative sacraments. From this viewpoint, then, there is no difference between the real presence of Jesus in the church and in each and all of the sacraments." op. cit., 207.

20. Mark Searle notes: "One of the major contributions of the RCIA to Catholic life and to sacramental theory is the way in which it has forced us to break with an almost magical understanding of the sacraments as discrete moments of divine intervention and to adopt a more flexible understanding of sacramentality as a process admitting of degrees. In this latter perspective the temporal duration of the catechumenal process, the various stages in the journey of faith undertaken by the candidates, the various ritual celebrations that mark the way culminating in the solemn Easter rites of baptism, confirmation and eucharist are all sacramental in varying degrees. The liturgy of the Easter Vigil is less the setting for three dis-

crete sacramental 'moments' than it is the climax of a process that is sacramental in its entirety." "Infant Baptism Reconsidered," *Baptism and Confirmation: Alternative Futures for Worship* (Collegeville: The Liturgical Press, 1987), 29.

21. Cf. James Fowler, *Becoming Adult, Becoming Christian* (San Francisco: Harper and Row, 1984); George Gallup and Jim Castelli, *The American Catholic People: Their Beliefs, Practices and Values* (Garden City, NY: Doubleday, 1987), 193; Dean R. Hoge, Joseph J. Shields, Mary Jeanne Verdieck, "Changing Age Distribution and Theological Attitudes of Catholic Priests, 1970–85" (Washington DC: Catholic University of America, 1987).

22. Cf. Philip J. McBrien, "Using the Lectionary as Our Textbook: Programs for Children and Their Teachers," *PACE* 17 (Winona MN: St. Mary's Press, 1986–87).

23. Andrew Thompson, "Infant Baptism and the Human Sciences" in Searle, op. cit., 92.

24. Sam Keen, *The Passionate Life: Stages of Loving* (New York: Harper and Row, 1983).

25. "It is crucial to realize that the introduction of children into an 'unprepared community' can be damaging. An 'unprepared community' is marked by national, ethnic, racial, economic, social and other divisions which are properties of this fallen world, totally alien to the community of the new age of God's kingdom." From "Eucharist with Children: Report of the Bad Segeberg Consultation," in Geiko Müller-Fahrenholz, ed., *And Do Not Hinder Them* (Geneva: World Council of Churches, 1982), 12. On a positive note, Aidan Kavanagh tells of the impact of the community's story: "Story chooses from the welter of facts certain events of importance in the cultural memory and then raises these to the level of analogies for the present. . . . Rooting us into the soil of a community story, these analogies do for us roughly what instinct does for animals; they help us survive by telling us in myriad ways . . . who we are in relation to all else. This is why tradition, another name for a culture's main business, is never merely

about past things but about the present within which a future is always begotten." *Confirmation: Origins and Reform* (New York: Pueblo, 1988), 116.

26. Herbert Anderson, "Pastoral Care in the Process of Initiation," in Searle, op. cit., 105.

27. Cf. canons 71, 842:2, 849, 879, 897; RCIA, 34; *Rite of Confirmation,* 11,13; Kavanagh, op. cit., 118.

28. Mark Searle, "Confirmation and the Church," *Assembly* 14:1 (September 1987), 384.

29. Ibid.

30. Cf. Kavanagh, op. cit., 104–06; Kenan Osborne agrees that "the mother lode of confirmation remains in and with the baptismal liturgy, so that what one says about baptism, with the exception of entry into the church, one says about confirmation." He adds that confirmation "takes one aspect of salvation that we celebrate in baptism, and revels in it." But he also states "the controlling issue [should] not be age, but the presence of the Spirit."

31. Kavanagh, op cit., 107.

Children's Initiation: Are We Ready?

JAMES B. DUNNING

Editor's note:
This article was an address given at the first Consultation on the Catechumenate for Children of Catechetical Age, December 4, 1988.

In this first consultation on the Christian initiation of children of catechetical age, sponsored by the North American Forum on the Catechumenate (Forum), I'll begin by situating children's initiation in relation to what we already have been doing with the adult catechumenate. I shall raise also two issues that form the backdrop of our discussion: the readiness of the parish and the readiness of families to receive and initiate children.

COMING AROUND FULL CIRCLE

This consultation brings us around full circle—from children to adults and back to children. It is fitting that the woman who started us on that circle, Christiane Brusselmans, is with us. Christiane studied the initiation of children at the Institut Catholique in Paris. Much to her surprise, the great French catechist Francois Coudreau told her first to spend several years with the adult catechumenate. That she did, and there she learned the dynamic of the catechumenate that places initiation within the community. Subsequently, she came to the United States, started a catechumenate for children in Washington, D.C., and later developed resources for the sacramental formation of children based on the catechumenate.

All that was prior to the 1972 publication of the *Rite of Christian Initiation of Adults* (RCIA) at a time when few parishes were ready to implement the catechumenate with adults.

In 1976 I was teaching sacramental theology at Seattle University. Christiane sat in on the course and intuited that what I was offering echoed the RCIA. She asked me if I had read that document. My response was like that of many of us back in 1976: "Why should I study 'our CIA'?" Two years later Christiane summoned me to France with 30 other Americans to share the French and African experience of the catechumenate. After that event, we began to offer institutes in North America. Forum was born. Now Forum gathers us to tap our experience with adults as we explore the initiation of children.

A note on language. Strictly speaking, there is no "RCIC" (Rite of Christian Initiation of Children). In the context of initiation, the Code of Canon Law (canon 852) sees children of catechetical age as adults. Here we view the implementation of the *Rite of Christian Initiation of Adults,* part II, chapter 1. It might be better to avoid one more acronym in the alphabet soup. Often people see the RCIA not as a sacramental order of the church but as one more program like CCD, CFM or RENEW. "RCIC" might suffer the same fate.

Paragraph 252 of the rite names the children about whom we speak, as Frank Sokol noted (see "Christian Initiation of Children: Introduction to the Text" in this volume): children not baptized as infants, children who have attained the use of reason and are of catechetical age, children presented by their parents/guardians or who present themselves with parental permission, children capable of a personal faith and the formation of conscience, children dependent on their parents/guardians and influenced by their companions.

Those criteria raise issues about the readiness of children. Since I've already discussed children's initiation in the previous article ("Let the Children Come to Me"), I'll raise only these two other important issues about readiness.

IS THE PARISH READY?

This is another way of stating Forum's one-liner, "Thou shalt not do to others what thou hast not done to thyself." With both adults and children we ask: If initiation takes place within the community (RCIA, 4) is the community on a conversion journey?

Another way to say it: After a decade of implementing the *Rite of Christian Initiation of Adults,* have parishes discovered their baptismal vocation, including the welcome and care of children? Regis Duffy claims some parishes are not ready for the RCIA because they aren't ready to receive anybody.

I'm convinced that we shall never renew sacramental actions, including initiation, until we become sacramental people, until we see a person's actions as the great sacraments. Vatican II named Jesus Christ crucified and risen as the primordial sacrament. His Spirit created a church that follows him and bears witness to him as the basic sacrament: a people. That people does not just receive, attend, say or see seven things. That people *does* seven big actions designated as the official sacraments of the church and seventy times seven other sacraments. In the catechumenate for adults and little adults, that people welcomes, signs with crosses, proclaims and listens to the word, dismisses (with great hospitality), calls and inscribes names, lays on hands, lights fires, immerses, anoints, eats and drinks.

Some parishes that do that seem ready to be sacraments. According to the Notre Dame study on the parish, 85 percent of Catholics believe the main purpose of baptism is not initiating into a community but forgiving original sin, 39 percent are concerned primarily with their own salvation, 21 percent with their salvation and also the common good. In a Gallup study, 34 percent of Catholics say sharing the love of Christ is important, and 41 percent encouraged others to believe in Jesus Christ.

Both big and little adults must meet those apathetic people especially at eucharist, at meals. Jesus put children at center stage. At eucharist we often keep them offstage. Robert Hovda writes of eucharist:

> Where else in our society are we all addressed and sprinkled and bowed to and incensed and touched and kissed and treated like *somebody*—all in the very same way? Where else do economic czars and beggars get the same treatment? Where else are food and drink blessed in a common prayer of thanksgiving, broken and poured out, so that everybody shares and shares alike? (*Liturgy* 80 [June/July 1982], 6)

Often we fail to treat children like unique somebodies. Often we fail to evangelize them, proclaim to them the good news. We "misangelize" them with bad news: badly worded comments in the liturgies, bad rites, bad music, bad art, bad spiritual and bad apostolic example, bad use of worship space. Especially at eucharist, children receive mixed messages from lethargic adults. This is a problem for all new members but a special problem for children, especially older children sensitive to hypocrisy.

We claim that the best way to invite the parish to be sacrament is through the galaxy of rites and the small communities of faith that are the catechumenate. It is not just one more renewal program. It is a sacramental action of our church. It is the way we initiate and become disciples of Christ.

IS THE FAMILY READY?

If the family is the domestic church, then the family also is sacrament. Is the family ready to welcome another member?

When asked to name things that harm family ministry, we first need to address the lack of attention given by catechumenate ministers to the spouses and families of candidates. Over 80 percent of those joining us do so for marital or family reasons. Do we uncover that as part of "their story"? Others joining us, especially from fundamentalist communities, often face enormous pain in their families. In an effort to be attentive to these issues, Forum has made contact with the National Association of Catholic Diocesan Family Life Ministers. We need to be sensitive to the principles of "A Family Perspective in Church and Society," published by the USCC in 1988.

We need to ask, if the journey of initiation effects deep cognitive, affective or behavioral change in one spouse, then what happens to the other? What happens to children, especially adolescents, when a parent suddenly "gets religion"? How can we involve families of both candidates and sponsors in the journey?

Recent research on family systems raises some new questions for us. Rabbi Edwin Friedman writes primarily about death, marriage and birth as rites of passage. If the catechumenate journey, however, is a rite of passage, especially for candidates who join us because of death, marriage or birth, might his words apply to us?

> [Ministers are very important] in families during rites of passage. . . . These rites are the most advantageous moments for entering and changing any family system. Life-cycle events are "hinges of time" on which doors can open or close for generations. . . . It is the family itself that is going through the passage, rather than only some "identified" celebrant(s), and the family actually may go through more change than the focused members do. . . . The attitudes of a family member will never change through a direct confrontation on ideological or cultural issues. On the contrary, these approaches always intensify the deeper emotional issues. (*Generation to Generation,* 5, 6, 165, 180)

If education means religious knowledge, parents usually are not the primary educators. They are, however, the first evangelizers and catechizers, if evangelization means experiencing the good news of God's love and if catechesis means echoing that good news. That good news came first not in words but a person, Jesus, God's word—in Hebrew, God's *dabar* (God's word-deed). That *dabar* continues to take flesh in persons, especially parents as the primary *dabar.*

PARISH AND FAMILY AS SACRAMENT

What the United States bishops said about all sacramental symbols is true of parents and other early adult models: Good symbols build faith, and bad symbols destroy faith. Readiness raises enormous questions about a child's family history and relationships, the images the child has received of God as Father or Mother.

Andrew Greeley's research on religious imagination affirms that people as sacraments, especially parents, are the context in which children can come to a high "grace scale," that is, a positive, hopeful view of life as gift. Greeley also gives hope to catechists when he observes that there is no correlation between this grace scale and years in Catholic schools or CCD, but there is a high correlation when a child has experienced a personal relationship with one good teacher (or catechist or sponsor). If a child's parents are not supportive or even if they have been abusive and did not work *ex opere operato* as sacraments of God's care, how might we offer to children those other important adults and companions as sacraments?

I'll close with a reminder that like catechumens, parish people and family people are elected—not perfected—as sacraments. Talk of readiness might paralyze us if we forget that the elect are elite not because they are sinless but because we know our sins, our fragility, our brokenness. That is how we share the good news of God's love. We proclaim that God loves us and calls us to be sacraments of that love to all who are broken. In *The Second Coming,* Walker Percy offers gripping images of broken sacraments. The book's main character, Will Barrett, is not saved from madness by friends, lovers, social position, wealth and especially not by his yuppie pastor. He hears the good news, and Christ comes again in a frail old missionary and in a strange, psychotic young woman who becomes his wife. According to the last lines of the novel,

> Will Barrett stopped the old priest at the door and gazed into his face. The bad eye spun and the good eye looked back at him fearful: What do you want of me? What do I want of him, mused Will Barrett and suddenly realized he had gripped the old man's wrists as if he were a child. The bones were like dry sticks. . . . Will Barrett thought about Allie in her greenhouse. . . . His heart leapt with a secret joy. What is it I want from her and him, he wondered, not only want but must have? Is she a gift and therefore a sign of a giver? Could it be that the Lord is here, masquerading behind this simple silly holy face? Am I crazy to want both, her and Him? No, not want, must have. Will have.

We hope the silly faces of our parishes and families are ready when Will, in the person of big or little adults, comes for initiation.

The Christian Initiation of Children

CHRISTIANE BRUSSELMANS

In the Fall of 1960, I found myself seeking a center where I could study pastoral catechetics and liturgy. Four years of theological studies at the Catholic University of Louvain (Belgium) and a dissertation on "Sponsorship and Infant Baptism during the First Four Centuries of the Church," not to mention non-stop celebration of infant baptism of 58 nephews and nieces, gave me a deep yearning to develop better ways to incorporate children in the sacramental life of the church.

My questions and concerns were the following: Where shall I find parishes who take the sacramental initiation of children seriously? What is the role of the parish community? What is the role of the parents? What is the role of the godparents? What is the role of the catechists? What is the role of the clergy? How do all these ministries complement one another? Which are the criteria for accepting an infant for baptism? Do parishes offer a prebaptismal formation to the parents? How do parents exercise their parental ministry?

It is with these questions and many other concerns, which I could not formulate at the time, that I visited Paris to have an interview with Father Francois Coudreau, the dynamic and visionary director of the Institut Catholique in Paris. It is to this institute that the French bishops since 1950 were sending their future directors of religious education and of liturgy.

I had a memorable interview with Father Coudreau. His response to my questions and concerns was: "I strongly urge you to leave your concerns with infant baptism 'in limbo' (i.e., on the threshold)." He also recommended that I do my fieldwork, at least for an entire year, in one of the 63 catechumenate centers for adults which were at that time functioning in the diocese of Paris (We are in 1960!). He urged me to take the time to immerse myself in the experience and assured me that after evaluating my pastoral experience I would discover the model and the principles which should govern the adaptation of the rites of Christian initiation of adults to the Christian initiation of children.

A radical conversion of mind and practice was required on my part. It took me nine years in parishes of varying cultural backgrounds in Washington, in New York and in Brussels to develop and experiment with a catechumenal model for the Christian initiation of children into the eucharist.

CHALLENGES TO SACRAMENTAL PRACTICE

In 1976, Aidan Kavanagh published *Made Not Born* (University of Notre Dame Press). In his book, Kavanagh claims that with the promulgation in Rome of the *Rite of Christian Initiation of Adults* (1972), the catechumenate became the *norm* for the sacramental practice of the church. Amen! The implications of this statement are mind-blowing.

A new ecclesiology is slowly emerging from the pastoral praxis for the Christian initiation not only of adults but also of youth, children and infants. No longer can the rite of infant baptism be the norm and model for Christian initiation at other ages. If this principle is valid then we must challenge a few sacramental practices.

1. The Sequence of the Sacraments of Initiation. All recent church documents request that the traditional sequence of the sacraments be restored in the following order: baptism, confirmation and eucharist. The tradition is expressed in the *Rite of Christian Initiation of Adults* (Roman), paragraphs 215, 216 and 217:

> In accord with the ancient practice followed in the Roman liturgy, adults are not to be baptized without receiving confirmation immediately afterwards. . . . Confirmation is conferred after the explanatory rites of baptism. . . . Finally, in the celebration of the eucharist, as they take part for the first time and with full right, the newly baptized reach the culminating point in their Christian initiation.

The *Code of Canon Law* (1983) promotes the same tradition and vision:

> The sacraments of baptism, confirmation and the blessed eucharist so complement one another that all three are required for full Christian initiation. (canon 842.2)

> Unless there is a grave reason to the contrary, immediately after receiving baptism an adult is to be confirmed, to participate in the celebration of the eucharist and to receive holy communion. (canon 866)

The *Rite of Christian Initiation of Adults* devotes a whole chapter to the "Christian Initiation of Children of Who Have Reached Catechetical Age." The church requests that the same sequence for the sacramental initiation of these children—baptism, confirmation and eucharist—be respected (#305).

The same sequence for the sacraments of initiation has also been endorsed by the bishops of the United States. In their *National Catechetical Directory* the two first paragraphs of chapter 6 on the sacraments states:

> Christian initiation is celebrated in baptism, confirmation or chrismation, and eucharist. Through these visible actions a person is incorporated into the church and shares its mission in the world. Baptism and confirmation (chrismation) enable recipients, through sharing in Christ's priestly office, to be intimately associated in the offering of the sacrifice of the eucharist.

Having affirmed the sequence and the unity of the sacraments of initiation the *Directory* points to the RCIA as being the norm:

> Full initiation into the church occurs by stages. The *Rite of Christian Initiation of Adults* provides a norm for catechetical as well as liturgical practice in this regard. (#115)

Despite the liturgical and the canonical law of the church as well as the teaching of the bishops of the United States, it is my experience that parishes which have restored the catechumenate for adults are still hesitant to start a catechumenate for children of catechetical age or use the RCIA as a norm and model for the full sacramental initiation of children and youth.

2. Shall We Continue to Baptize Infants? Yes, of course! When the church states that the *Rite of Christian Initiation of Adults* is the norm, this certainly does not mean that the practice of infant baptism is obsolete. Infant baptism is an ecclesial tradition that developed during the first decades of the existence of the church. When pagan or Jewish converts asked for baptism, many brought their whole household with them. This practice is based on their concept of family solidarity and by the authority which was exercised by the *paterfamilias*. This seems to be the case with Cornelius' entrance into the church (Acts 10:44), and also with that of Stephanas (1 Corinthians 1:16).

As it is demonstrated through the structure and the discipline of the catechumenate in the third century, faith and the conversion of the adult candidate is at the heart of the infant's admission to the sacraments of initiation. Therefore, the justification of the practice of infant baptism is founded on the faith and the conversion of the Christian parents and the guarantee that their child will be nourished by the parents in the Christian faith. What is being challenged by the restoration of the RCIA is not infant baptism but indiscriminate baptism of both adults and infants.

The Vatican *Instruction on Infant Baptism* (1980) urges pastors and parish ministers to seek well-founded assurances that children who are being baptized grow up in an environment conducive to growth in the Catholic faith. Experience shows that parishes and parents who have experienced the stages and the steps of the RCIA will have a much easier time adapting and enriching their parish baptismal programs for infants. A longer delay of some cases is being proposed by the Roman instruction on infant baptism, especially for parents who are weak in their faith and need a time of preparation.

A few characteristics which infant baptismal preparation can borrow from the RCIA model are:

1. Let there be a baptismal team and ministry.
2. Let there be evangelization.
3. Let there be time for a baptismal catechesis.
4. Let there be celebrations (steps and stages).
5. Let there be ministries: parents as sponsors, godparents, catechists, parish priests.
6. Let there be time for conversion.
7. Let there be discernment of motivations.

It is to be hoped that we will be allowed to restore stages and periods for the baptismal preparation of infants. I see no reason why the baptismal preparation of the parents who present their infants for infant baptism could not follow the principles and norms which the RCIA applies to adults and to children of catechetical age (seven years). If we succeed at taking those steps, the baptism of infants will no longer be a private and unprepared affair on a Sunday afternoon but could become for many the beginning of a lifelong commitment to the church and to ministering in the church. Towards this end catechists and liturgists suggest that there be quarterly or monthly communal celebrations of infant baptism.

The RCIA does not hesitate to take radical steps, as can be seen in chapter 1 of part II, which deals with children of catechetical age:

> As with adults, [children's] initiation is to be extended over several years, if need be, before they receive the sacraments. . . . Their initiation is marked by several steps. (#253)

3. Who Are the Sponsors of Infant Baptism? Recently, I attended the baptism of an infant who was presented by his parents for incorporation into the parish community. All the liturgical functions of the sponsors were carried out by the parents of the infant:

- presenting their child to the community
- giving of a Christian name
- making the signation
- profession of renunciations
- proclamation of the baptismal creed
- holding the child over the baptismal font
- receiving the lighted candle

During the whole celebration, godfather and godmother were standing by. It was clear that they represented the church and that they would help the child or his parents whenever help would be needed. Nobody was going to deprive the parents of their primary ministry to their child.

I am giving you this short description of the liturgical rites because pastors and directors of sacramental programs might be confused by the English translation given to the ministry of the sponsor in the English text of the *Code of Canon Law*. The 1983 code has an entire chapter on the sponsor (Canons 872, 873, 874). The latter canon is the one in question here. It says:

> To be admitted to the role of sponsor a person must not be the father or the mother of the one to be baptized. (canon 874.5)

Ministers engaged in the sacramental initiation of infants and of children of catechetical age can readily see how this canon contradicts all their efforts to have parents resume their ministry of sponsoring their children. I consulted Rev. Bertram Griffin from the Portland (Oregon) Tribunal. He immediately saw the error and told me (1) always to look up the Latin text, which is the only official text of the church's law, and (2) to compare the Latin word with the English translation. In the Latin text the word used in all the previously listed canons is *padrini*. The English translation of *padrini* is "godparent." This is sufficient to make me happy. Parents are the sponsors. Godparents will assist them.

4. What about Confirmation? The May 1986 issue of the *Chicago Catechumenate* has an article from Terri McKenzie and Michael Savelsky. The title of the article might sound odd to many. To me it makes a lot of sense: "Confirmation with First Communion? It works." Two parishes that I know of in Spokane, Washington—St. Peter and Our Lady of Fatima—have chosen to restore the traditional and normative way for the celebration of the sacraments of initiation for children: baptism, confirmation and eucharist. As a preliminary step for implementing this sequence for the initiation of children preparing for communion, a vibrant adult catechumenate has prepared the way and given to the parish a visible model of what Christian initiation can be.

Building on their experiences of the RCIA, a leadership group conducted a study mandated by the Bishop of Spokane. The study group concluded:

> In accordance with church teaching, tradition and law, the sequential and liturgical integration of baptism, confirmation and eucharist should be restored as norm [in their parishes].

In granting his approval the bishop stated:

> It is my fond desire as bishop that these sacraments (baptism, confirmation and eucharist) be seen and lived in relationship to one another as the church intends them to be.

The bishop also cautioned the parishes to manifest pastoral sensitivity to those parishioners who might be disturbed by this development either because of lack of understanding or because of their own experience of confirmation. Some of the expected motivations and concerns of the parishioners were:

- the feeling that a sacrament (confirmation) is needed to keep the older child in religious education classes
- the need to give youth an opportunity to make an adult commitment to their Christian life

- the need to assist youth in their search for maturity

Finally, the leadership group saw the necessity of the bishop's presence for the sacramental celebration of the completion of Christian initiation (confirmation and first eucharist).

I have extensively quoted the report of the Spokane initiation experience because I am convinced that it works and that the tradition of the church, which has been restated in all church documents promulgated after the Second Vatican Council, is very sound.

Other similar experiences are being carried on. Reverend Richard Moudry, pastor of Christ the King Parish in St. Paul-Minneapolis, has opted for the restoration of the traditional sequence for the Christian initiation of children in his parish (See "A Parish Experience" by Richard Moudry, in this book).

What seems important to me is that decisions be made after a careful study has been done of the tradition and the general law of the church as well as the principles and liturgical norms outlined in the *Rite of Christian Initiation of Adults*. In order for this to happen, I would hope that future diocesan guidelines for the sacraments of initiation would allow for pluralism and that the bishops would permit experimentation with confirmation at a later age (maturity model) as well as the earlier age (initiation model). Pluralism does not have to be seen as a negative but rather as a healthy tension out of which good sacramental practice will emerge.

In those parishes where the "initiation model" is the norm, religious education and youth ministers will have to meet the religious needs of the youth. While this remains a challenge to many parishes, it also represents a call to develop catechesis and rites that more appropriately celebrate the stages of our young adults.

5. Initiation into the Eucharist Parishes in the United States, Canada, England, Australia and New Zealand have increasingly adopted a catechumenal model for the Christian initiation of children into the eucharist. The results and evaluation of this approach are most encouraging:

1. Many parish leaders have discovered the existence of the *Rite of Christian Initiation of Adults* through the experience of a first communion preparation.

2. Ministries have been entrusted to parents, to godparents, to prayer companions, to catechists, to liturgical ministers (the artists) and to the parish priest. The variety and the complementarity of these ministries has brought new life and creativity to the parish.

3. The approach is family- and parish-centered, with the active support of the Catholic school and catechists.

4. Time has been a very important factor. A nine-month journey for the children and their parents allows for a genuine initiation of the children and in many cases evangelization and conversion of many parents.

5. Celebrations are the climax of each month's catechesis given to the children and, hopefully, to the parents. The celebration in such programs offers adaptations of the rites in the RCIA in such a way that children, their parents, and other members of the family or of the community can actively participate.

6. It is a way for parents and for the members of the extended family to discover the ministries and the call to mission in the Christian community.

A Parish Experience

RICHARD P. MOUDRY

Ideally, the way a parish community practices pastoral ministry reflects an integrated vision of church life. Ideally, the way a parish initiates has an internal consistency, whether the initiates are adults or children, unbaptized or baptized. The various pastoral ministries of a parish are in dialogue with each other. The various initiating ministries of a parish also speak to one another. The result of this reverberation can be mutual harmony and support, or the result can be inconsistency.

FROM DISSONANCE TO HARMONY

Let me tell you about what happened in our parish, about the way our parish initiates children as a result of earlier inconsistencies in our parish initiation practices.

At Christ the King Parish in Minneapolis, we implemented the *Rite of Christian Initiation of Adults* (RCIA) in our ministry to adults before we implemented the catechumenate for children. In fact, I don't remember our having many unbaptized children of catechetical age in the early 1970s. Those we had we dealt with on an individual basis. One memory stands out:

In 1976, the religious education director of our parish and her husband adopted two Korean children who were of catechetical age. When it was time, we celebrated their initiation fully: baptism, confirmation and first communion, all together in the same liturgy. A first for our parish and a first for me. Actually, for us the parish-wide implementation of the order of Christian initiation began in 1978 with the establishment of a catechumenate.

In the late 1970s, many parishes in our part of the country started to "do something" about the sacrament of confirmation. "Doing something" then meant moving confirmation from about the seventh grade (our parish practice) to the high school years and making the sacrament the centerpiece of a parish religious education or youth program for teenagers. Should we follow suit?

We were already beginning to feel the inconsistency between our practice of adult initiation and our practice of completing the initiation of our already-baptized Catholic children. Because of that inconsistency, we decided not to follow the high-school confirmation trend but, instead, to take a first step toward harmonizing our parish initiation practices. We changed the age of confirmation for our Catholic children. Beginning in 1982, the children of the age of reason in our parish began receiving confirmation and first communion from the bishop at the same Mass. The completion of their Christian initiation followed the catechumenate model: traditional sequence, earlier age, unified celebration.

Looking back (this article was written in the eighth year of our parish practice) it doesn't seem such a great step to have taken. But in 1982 it looked like a major change, and it felt risky.

As a pastor, I am struck by two features of our change. First, the catechumenate for adults and then for unbaptized children of catechetical age called us to revise the way we were completing the initiation of our Catholic children, bringing it into greater harmony with the *Rite of Christian Initiation of Adults*. Second, it was this change in the way we initiated our Catholic children that really drew the attention of our parish community to the Second Vatican Council's reform of Christian initiation. The catechumenate has had its greatest impact on our parish not when we established it for adults and not when we struggled to provide a children's catechumenate, but when we changed the way we completed the initiation of the much larger group of baptized children of our most faithful, steadfast and outspoken Catholic families.

STEP BY STEP

Here is how we went about introducing this change to the parents of Catholic children of first-communion age. The first year, 1982–83, and every year since, I met with the parents and as their pastor explained the new policy and the rationale for the change. Let me outline the main points of the rationale I offered:

1. Unified Rite. What we today know as the separate sacraments of baptism, first communion and confirmation were, in their origins, a single, unified rite of initiation that included a water bath, anointing with imposition of hands and full participation in the eucharist. For centuries this was the norm and remained the practice in Rome until the thirteenth century for adults and for children.

2. Three Sacraments Complete Initiation. Originally, the three symbols—bath, anointing, meal—celebrated one reality: full entrance into the paschal assembly, becoming members, conversion, initiation. All three rites together—baptism, confirmation and first communion—are initiation.

3. Historical Fragmentation. Gradually and for reasons having nothing to do with the meaning of Christian initiation, the three symbols became separated: First, baptism came to be celebrated without confirmation; later baptism came to be celebrated without first communion. The resulting fragmentation of Christian initiation was part of a larger picture of Catholic sacramental life that today we acknowledge is in decline.

4. Persistent Sense of Faith. Even after the fragmentation, the sense of the faithful continued to draw the three sacraments into a coherent initiatory whole. The popular instinct was that confirmation and first communion belonged back with baptism. When baptism came to be celebrated alone, the faithful would seek to have the newly baptized confirmed and given first communion as soon as possible afterwards. That centripetal or uniting dynamic can be seen to this day in Latin cultures, in Catholic regions less influenced by the Protestant Reformation.

5. Two-step Practice. By the early Middle Ages, a two-step practice of initiating Catholic children had emerged: baptism at infancy completed by confirmation and first communion at about the age of seven. The association of first communion with age seven came about not so much to set an age for admission to the eucharist but to identify the age at which the baptized incurred the obligations to receive communion. In fact, the practice of communicating infants and toddlers persisted in some parts of the Catholic world well into the sixteenth century.

6. Emphasis Shifts from Rite to Instruction. It was largely as a result of the Protestant Reformation that confirmation and first communion came to be celebrated as Counter-Reformation catechetical events, stages of childhood instruction in a basically apologetic faith.

7. Out of Order. We are probably the first generation of Catholics in history able to imagine celebrating first communion before confirmation as the rule. Not until Pius X at the start of the present century did confirmation swing out of order to an age later than first communion. This deviation was permitted by church authorities by way of exception, so that more difficult access to episcopal confirmation would not stand in the way of early first communion. After a few decades, this "exceptional" practice became so common that we have come in our day to imagine it to be the Catholic way.

8. Recent Popular Trends. The widespread practice of moving confirmation to high-school years and the development of a rationale for that shift took place in the 1970s and early 1980s. The new practice and its rationale were virtually untouched by the Vatican II reform of Christian initiation. The *Rite of Christian Initiation of Adults* was promulgated in 1972, and our English translation was approved in 1975. Only now, at the end of the 1980s, is high-school confirmation being critiqued in light of the liturgical theology of the RCIA and out of parish experience of adult and children's catechumenates and combined sacramental celebrations of initiation. In a word, high-school confirmation is a pre–Vatican II phenomenon.

9. The Order Is Restored. As a result of the Second Vatican Council, Christian initiation was reformed in ministering to unbaptized adults, unbaptized children of catechetical age, baptized Protestants and Catholics who are uncatechized and baptized Christians seeking full communion with the Catholic church. In this reform, baptism, confirmation and eucharist are celebrated as initiation rites in that order and always together.

10. Two-step Practice Reaffirmed. But for children born to practicing Catholic parents, no similar reform of initiation emerged from the Second Vatican Council. Rather, for them the two-step practice of children's initiation, dating back to the early Middle Ages, was reaffirmed: They were baptized in infancy, later confirmed and given first communion at the age of reason. The fragmentation was unremedied, and the recent anomaly of confirmation after first communion was not addressed.

THE PARISH RESPONSE

After explaining this rationale, I proposed to parents our parish policy: Instead of joining the movement toward later, high-school confirmation, at Christ the King we implement the two-step practice that has been affirmed by Vatican II. For parents, that means your seven-year-old child will be confirmed and given first communion from the bishop when he visits our parish. Even though this practice is not a reform, it restores for us the sequence of the initiation rites and makes first communion, not confirmation, the culmination of Christian initiation. It is less inconsistent with the Vatican II reform.

How did the Catholic parents of our parish react to the new practice? In the first year, 1982, a few of our most committed and devout parents objected to the change. Their reasons were sincere and fell into three categories: 1) We want more, not fewer, occasions for additional religious instruction of our children. 2) Our little second graders are not old enough to understand and undertake what is necessary for confirmation. 3) We want these two special days, First Communion Day and Confirmation Day, to be kept separate so that they will remain two powerful childhood memories. In response, that first year we had extra meetings with the reluctant parents. To help them cope with the change, we discussed the two differing images of confirmation—as a catechetical event and as an initiatory event—images that are played out with differing expectations and practices.

In the end, given the choice that first year, more than 80 percent of that first group of parents chose to have their second grader confirmed at their first communion Mass. To catch up, some families had two or three other children confirmed that year in addition to their first communicant.

After the second year of the new practice, we dropped the language of "invitation" and "option." We presented the combined rite as parish practice and dealt with troubled parents on an individual basis. Since the third year, parents have not objected. Confirmation with first communion is simply parish practice at Christ the King.

LOOKING BACK

Our seven years of parish experience with early and combined confirmation and first communion has taught me some lessons. I will identify three. First, when initiation was completed early, I found that children did not drop out of religious education classes as in the past. Parents did not remove the children from our parish school or CCD classes after confirmation and first communion in the second grade. Enrollment in religious education classes at the junior-high level has increased over the past seven years of early confirmation.

Second, when it was the parish that initiated and not just the parish school or CCD, I was able more clearly to distinguish initiation from religious education, which is rightly concerned with curriculum scope and sequence, instructional settings and "content." Religious education remains the responsibility of our parish education ministries, but those ministries do not conduct the initiation of the children of our parish. As we ready children for confirmation and first communion, we are not engaged in "sacramental preparation" in the sense of the term that has come to us from the days of preparing children for childhood sacraments in the parish school or CCD. We found that in our parish, "sacramental preparation" was a school mindset, an educational assumption that persons who were to be initiated needed education in advance, needed to complete curricula and gain understandings before their initiation. I found the term "sacramental preparation" a handicap in exploring the meaning of initiation.

Third, by focusing on confirmation and first communion as initiatory events and by completing initiation early, the shape of parish ministry was clarified for me. When a parish community decides to initiate, the parish commits itself to those being initiated. When parents choose to have a baby, with that childbirth or "initiation" comes an agenda of decades of parenting responsibilities to their child or "neophyte." Similarly, when a parish initiates, whether it be adults or children, when the initiation is completed, the community then undertakes to minister to the initiated by "traditioning," continued formation, catechesis and religious education, Catholic socialization, youth ministry and adult education. All these parish ministries are post-initiatory ministries; they derive from Christian initiation and are built upon it.

OBSERVATIONS

Our parish experience of completing the initiation of baptized children at an early age accounts for my discomfort with some recommendations proposed for implementing the children's catechumenate. For example, the concern in the rite itself for the emotional comfort of the child catechumens strikes me as exaggerated. We have not found children to be intimidated by the parish assembly. I question that we should celebrate principal catechumenal liturgies (acceptance, election and scrutiny) apart from the Sunday assembly just because the catechumens are children.

I am saddened that the children's catechumenate seems to have become another arena for promoting first confession before first communion for Catholic children. First confession is more strongly promoted in the 1988 United States revision of the *Rite of Christian Initiation of Adults* than in the original 1972 text. The text of the children's scrutiny (penitential) rite already tends to eviscerate and domesticate the conflict between the power of God in Jesus the Lord and the powers of evil that is at the heart of a catechumenal scrutiny. To structure the scrutiny as a group preparation for the celebration of the first confession further trivializes the nature of the evil that the church names and targets for assault in a scrutiny. As a final anomaly: The catechumens being "scrutinized" end up as silent spectators while other children make their first confession in a sacramental service tacked on to the end of the scrutiny.

One sometimes hears the language of Christian initiation, such as "mystagogy," to describe ecclesial ministries to children long after their initiation is completed. As understood in the RCIA, Christian initiation is not open-ended, flowing over into Christian life in general.

These days it is conventional to assert that the RCIA implemented for adults is "normative" and that all other Christian initiation ministry should be carried out in light of it. When it comes to the initiation of children of catechetical age, the adult rite is helpful in ministering to older children, adolescents and teenagers. But when we minister to younger children, from about age six to ten, we can benefit from also looking in the opposite direction, at infant baptism. Our parish experience suggests that a second grader is as much an older version of an infant as a younger version of an adult. When we initiate a child of seven, for example, we can benefit by exploring what initiatory realities such as "conversion," "initiation" and "membership" mean when we baptize a newborn.

Our parish experience of early completion of initiation may be a useful contribution to the larger discussion of children's initiation. But if our kind of experience is to contribute to the discussion, it would be helpful if diocesan guidelines did not mandate high-school age confirmation to the exclusion of the earlier two-step initiation practice found in the documents of Vatican II. Unfortunately, in 1972 the National Conference of Catholic Bishops (NCCB) moved swiftly to authorize deviation from the earlier age of confirmation in the general law before the RCIA was even promulgated, reinforcing the dichotomy between our practices of initiating children and adults. If you are in a position to influence policy in your home diocese, I urge you to seek diocesan sacramental guidelines that allow early initiation—confirmation along with first communion at age seven—at least as an exception, or, better, an option, or, still better, as a diocesan policy to which later confirmation is the exception.

CONCLUSION

I would like to close on a note of challenge for all of us. Let me confess, I am more and more dissatisfied with the practice of early initiation that I have described for you and that I do not hesitate to recommend to you. Seven years of parish experience with early initiation of our Catholic children only intensifies my conviction that, while it may serve as a first step in the right direction, in the end it is inadequate and unsatisfactory. Why? It is still too inconsistent with the overall reform of Christian initiation.

I believe that the overarching goal of the liturgical reform of the Second Vatican Council was to foster paschal piety—our parishioners knowing, celebrating and living the paschal mystery. The paschal season was reformed with the Easter Triduum as its centerpiece. Further, Sunday was restored to its preeminent role as the premier paschal observance, with the Sunday eucharist functioning as the weekly renewal of the paschal mystery in our local churches. Still further, baptism, confirmation and first communion were reformed as sacraments of initiation that together celebrate and proclaim the action of our triune God in the birthing of a church of disciples for the transformation of society. Those who are initiated experience the paschal reality: They are raised up by the Father out of their death in the Lord and are "membered" in the Spirit community of the church. One paschal and trinitarian reality, celebrated as one: baptism, confirmation and first communion together. The *Rite of Christian Initiation of Adults* holds out the hope that a local church that initiates with these reformed rites will itself be gradually renewed in paschal piety.

Yet, in the face of the grand paschal vision of Vatican II, we continue to celebrate Christian initiation 95 percent of the time, with our Catholic children, in a fragmented way, clearly inconsistent with the integrity of the redemptive paschal mystery it proclaims. How can we continue to justify depriving baptized persons of full participation in the eucharist? Because they are just infants? How can we continue to celebrate confirmation apart from baptism? That practice is no longer innocuous. It is harmful. Baptism apart from confirmation is already strictly forbidden when initiating anyone of at least catechetical age, and this for reasons central to the meaning of the paschal mystery (RCIA, 215). Is the paschal significance to be less relevant when we are initiating infants?

The direction of the reform is clear: Whenever the church initiates, whether infants, children of catechetical age, teenagers or adults, the celebration should be complete at the initiation event. Without confirmation and eucharist, Christian initiation is not complete.

The direction of the reform of Christian initiation is at least as clear today as the direction of the reform of the eucharist was in the 1960s. In those years, we set out to implement the reform of the eucharist, summoning our parishioners to the changes involved. In the 25 years since, we have dealt with all the trial and error involved in our growing into the eucharistic reform. Why such bold action? Because the direction was clear and the issue was central to our faith. Similarly, the direction of the reform of Christian initiation is clear today. The issue is at least as central to our faith.

The NCCB could take the key step—confirmation with baptism for all—at any time. The NCCB has already authorized individual bishops to act independently in choosing when to confirm. With the same authority used to allow or mandate high school confirmation, canon 891, which provides for a national conference to determine "another age" (than the age of discretion), bishops could allow or mandate confirmation with baptism for infants. That step would bring the initiation of our children into harmony with the overall reform of Christian initiation. The present inconsistency of our initiation practices would be remedied.

The result: The church in its entire initiation ministry will proclaim, celebrate and—we hope—live the paschal mystery with greater authenticity.

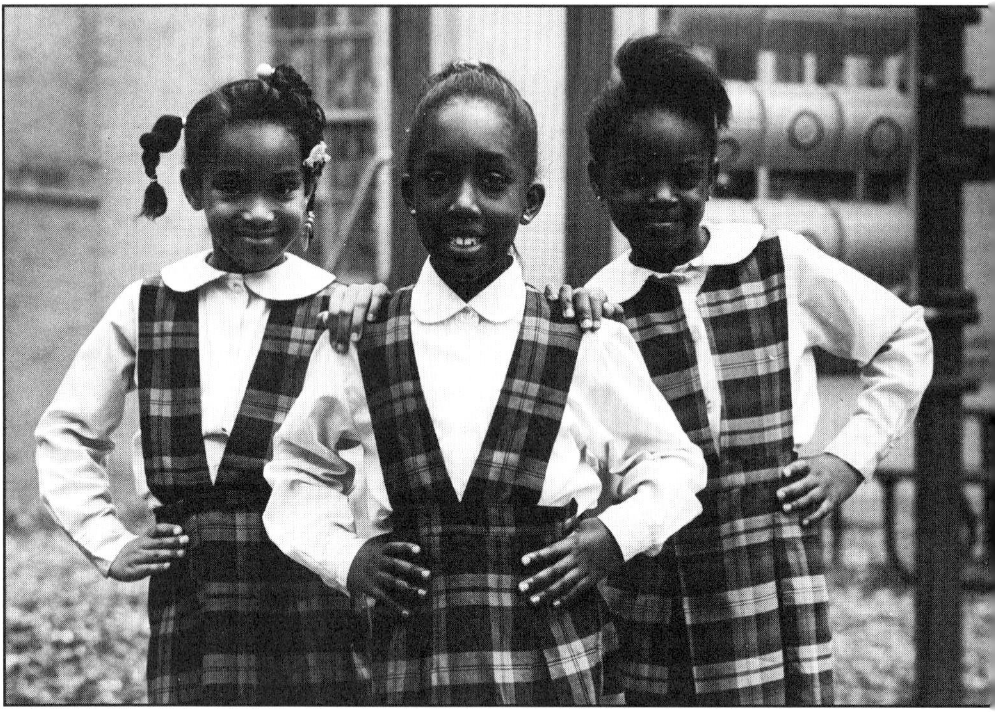

PART TWO:

Working with the Reformed Rite

Christian Initiation of Children: Introduction to the Text

FRANK C. SOKOL

Part II of the *Rite of Christian Initiation of Adults* (RCIA), approved for use in the dioceses of the United States, begins with a chapter devoted to the "Christian Initiation of Children Who Have Reached Catechetical Age" (CIC). Now that the implementation of part I (initiation of adults) is underway, theorists and practitioners are beginning to explore the "whys" and "hows" of the chapters contained in part II. The chapter on the initiation of children may well be the most controversial and revolutionary of all the directives set out in the RCIA because it is most challenging to many of our current sacramental practices for children. The catechumenate for children will lead us to investigate whether we are, in fact, initiating children into the life of a faith-filled community or merely dispensing sacraments.

The purpose of this article is to examine the *praenotanda,* that is, the paragraphs of introduction to the text of the rites for children, and to comment on the issues that are raised there. As such, this commentary will be limited to paragraphs 252 to 259 of the RCIA, which pertain to the initiation of children of catechetical age. These eight paragraphs serve as the backdrop for the rituals of the catechumenal process for children, and, in skeletal form, represent the primary shape for the initiation of children.

SUBJECTS OF THE RITE

Paragraph 252 sets out certain criteria that indicate for whom the rite is intended. These criteria are as follows:

- children not baptized as infants
- children who have attained the use of reason and are of catechetical age
- children presented by their parents/guardians, or who present themselves with parental permission
- children capable of a personal faith and the formation of conscience
- children dependent on their parents/guardians and influenced by their companions

The intention of the rite is to awaken and deepen the faith of children at a time when they are moving beyond their primary socialization in the home and when their lives are coming to include a larger circle of other significant adults and friends. This time of life is defined loosely as "the school years." They are school years because they mark a child's secondary socialization, when associations and interactions broaden beyond the home and exert a tremendous influence on development.

The potential catechumens could be children whose parents are also catechumens, children of Catholic parents who are returning to active membership after a period of inactivity, children of nonpracticing Catholic parents, children whose parents belong to other churches or to no church. Their curiosity about the church could be triggered by an association with school friends whose families practice their faith. This seems to be the reason that the CIC is designated for children *of catechetical age*.

The text further underlines the need for the development of faith and conscience. The language and symbols of the community of faith become the basis for gradually introducing the child into new ways of thinking and acting. The tradition of the church is the abundant banquet from which the catechumens are fed. The gradual awakening of the religious sense that is innate in the preschooler now needs greater focus and articulation in the language and symbols of the Catholic community.

PROCESS

Paragraph 253 describes the initiation of children in terms consistent with the initiation of adults. It is a process that must be adapted to a child's growth in faith. The conversion that is expected should be appropriate to a person's age. Thus, the CIC is set within the same framework as the RCIA proper. There is a gradual formation marked by ritual steps that continue even after initiation.

Because this is a gradual and ongoing process, the expectations can be realistic. Because it is a process of initiation, it focuses only on the beginning of the Christian life. This focus leaves room for more growth. There can be greater calm about all the segments of a lesson plan or about whether all the doctrines of the faith need to be covered *at the beginning,* at one's initiation. As the process continues, the totality of the Christian life and truth will be experienced.

With the necessary changes, the ritual steps and formational periods for children are parallel to the steps and periods outlined in the text for adult initiation. The formational process for children continues long after the sacraments of initiation are celebrated, as it does for adults.

COMPANIONS AND PARENTS

Paragraph 254 sets out one of the most insightful of all the directives. It affirms the indispensable role of children's companions in their journey of faith and, therefore, reiterates the basic premise of paragraph 4 of the RCIA: "The initiation of catechumens takes place within the community of the faithful." Where do catechumens belong? According to the text, they belong with their friends, who themselves may be preparing to complete their initiation through confirmation and eucharist.

This approach requires that the process be more than a cognitive one. If only knowledge were important, it would seem awkward to join catechumens with their baptized companions. However, along with the important dimension of knowledge, there are other aspects of formation in faith that are developed in and through the natural social groups to which children belong.

Special sessions, including the Sunday dismissal, can be scheduled for the catechumens so that their particular needs are addressed. Care should be taken in these settings that no more is expected of the unbaptized children than of their baptized peers. Sessions with their baptized companions, as well as for the unbaptized alone, will enhance their progress in the faith.

This paragraph calls also for parental support. In reality, however, this support is lacking sometimes. While they may give permission for their children to enter the church, parents sometimes do so without enthusiasm. The importance of companions in the faith in these cases is heightened, as is the role of sponsors. One source for sponsors might be the parents of the companions. Since their children are preparing to complete their initiation, these parents may be willing to nurture the faith of their children's unbaptized friends.

RITUAL STEPS

Paragraph 255 follows the preceding directive and calls for the rituals to be celebrated by "a group of several children who are in this same situation." Once again the significance of a community of peers is underlined. While this does not exclude the possibility of joining the children with the adult catechumens at times, the text acknowledges the advantages in adapting the celebrations for the community of children, both the baptized and the catechumens.

READINESS

Paragraph 256 raises the question of when the sacraments of initiation for children are to be celebrated. Preferably these would be scheduled for the Easter Vigil, with the rite of election (optional) and the penitential rites coinciding with Lent. This means that the children would join their adult counterparts in these celebrations.

This paragraph also raises the question of readiness by stating, "Before the children are admitted to the sacraments at Easter, it should be established that they are ready for the sacraments." Readiness is not easily definable. Usually it is not measured by the completion of a class program. Rather, it is noted in a sense of the holy that a catechumen may have and a willingness to enter into that mystery. The children themselves, in conversation and interaction with representatives of the community, with catechists, sponsors, parents and priests, will know when they are ready. This discernment occurs by reflecting on the actions of one's life as consistent or inconsistent with what is to be celebrated in each of the ritual stages. Consistency indicates at least basic readiness to proceed to the next period of Christian formation.

CELEBRATIONS WITH SMALLER GROUPS

Paragraph 257 recognizes that children may be intimidated by the presence of a very large community of people, most of whom they probably do not know. In such cases the celebrations should occur with a smaller group of family, friends, catechists, sponsors and representatives of the community. Other appropriate times for these rituals need to be found, such as the Sunday liturgy of the word for children, described in the *Directory for Masses with Children*. So that other children may participate, some liturgies may have to be planned for weekdays when the regular catechetical sessions take place.

ADAPTATION

Paragraph 258 not only allows for the adaptation of the rites for children, it directs that they "should be" adapted. The paragraph illustrates this directive by noting that the National Conference of Catholic Bishops has added an optional Rite of Election and Enrollment of Names for children. Particular attention is given here to the language that is used. The translations from the Latin text are to be understandable for children, and even an original alternative text may be written in order to provide greater comprehension.

The principle of adaptation—of the rites themselves and of the language within the rites—reflects a central dynamic of the entire catechumenal journey: that the people determine the process, that the catechumenal structure was created for people, not people for the structure.

Applying the principles of adaptation to children may seem quite simple but, in fact, it presents a substantial challenge. Especially because language reflects a vision of reality, care should be taken in the choice of words and images. A whole new way of seeing and acting is transmitted in the language which is used to invite, attract and challenge.

OPTIONS

Paragraph 259, the final of the *praenotanda*, respects the fact that what works well with one group may not be successful with another. It states that there should be "full and wise" use of options that allow the children, not the structure, to become the focus of the process. Becoming familiar with all available options enables the rituals to be living celebrations of the faith of the community. In the process of initiating children, options include the creative yet faithful implementation of the text.

IMPLICATIONS

These eight paragraphs offer a vision and direction that ensure the implementation of a successful catechumenate for children. They do not intend to set out a "how to." Rather, they provide a foundation upon which to build. They serve as a prolegomenon to the ecclesial enterprise of initiating the young into believing communities.

These comments on the *praenotanda* only begin to explore the richness of the church's way of forming children in the likeness of Christ. Further conversation and pastoral experience will show that these paragraphs from the text offer a model, not only for becoming a Christian, but also for remaining one.

Catechumenate for Children: Sharing the Gift of Faith

CATHERINE DOOLEY

It is becoming more and more common in parishes throughout the United States to have large numbers of children of school age who are unbaptized and uncatechized enroll in the parish programs of religious education.[1] One of the ways in which parishes meet the needs of these children is by implementing part II, chapter 1, of the *Rite of Christian Initiation of Adults,* the order of initiation for children of catechetical age.

The rites and the catechumenate for children is sometimes called the "RCIC," but this is a misnomer, since there is no separate rite for children; rather, in the ritual for adult initiation, the major rites of the catechumenate have been accommodated for children. While the texts of these rites have been simplified to the understanding of children, the norms for the implementation of the children's catechumenate are the principles of the *Rite of Christian Initiation of Adults.* This article will give an overview of the order for children,[2] indicate some areas of concern and explore some of the implications of the catechumenate for children of catechetical age for catechesis and sacramental practice.

CHILDREN'S CATECHUMENATE

The children's catechumenate is intended for those children who were not baptized as infants, who have attained the use of reason and are of catechetical age. The children are either brought by the parents or guardians or come of their own accord with parental permission to ask for initiation. "Such children are capable of receiving and nurturing a personal faith and of recognizing an obligation in conscience" (#252).[3]

The purpose of the catechumenate is to provide a means of conversion consonant with the child's age and understanding. The periods of the catechumenate—precatechumenate, catechumenate, enlightenment and mystagogia—are separated by whatever time is needed in order to deepen the faith of the child and to strengthen the efforts at conversion. The initiation may last for several years, depending upon the child's age and circumstances. The periods of initiation are marked by several steps or liturgical rites that indicate the catechumen's progress "as they pass, so to speak, through another doorway" on the journey of conversion. The three liturgical rites are acceptance as catechumens, rite of election and the sacraments of initiation.

Acceptance into the Order of Catechumens. As soon as the child is ready to request baptism, the rite of acceptance, followed by the liturgy of the word,[4] takes place. The parents (sponsors) give their assent to the preparation for baptism and they, together with the family and friends of the child, promise their help and support. The children are marked with the sign of the cross and are invited to take their place in the Christian assembly in the liturgy of the word. The book of the gospels may be presented to the child at this time. The rite of acceptance presumes a readiness to enter into the catechumenate. Depending upon the circumstances of the child, a precatechumenate may be needed for those who are uncatechized, in order to give a basic understanding of the Christian faith and life and to come to awareness of the meaning of initiation.[5]

Optional Rite of Election.[6]   The bishops of the United States included an optional rite of election that takes place at the beginning of Lent and marks the beginning of the time of the final preparation for the sacraments of initiation. The rite of election, or the enrollment of names, is termed optional simply because it does not appear in the "white book"—the official adaptation of the RCIA for use in the United States. The intent is that it will ordinarily be used. This celebration takes place during Mass in the cathedral church, parish church or, if necessary, some other suitable place. The presentation of the children occurs after the homily at the liturgy of the word.[7]

Special attention is given to calling each child by name, which concretizes the words of Isaiah 45:3, "That you may know that I am the Lord, the God of Israel, who calls you by your name," and emphasizes the meaning of God's election of each child. The rite of election presents in word and symbol the call and response that is the paradigm of the Christian life. The rite of being called by God through the Christian community places the focus on God's loving graciousness in their lives and heightens the children's awareness of the freedom to respond. The affirmation of the godparents and the community manifests this reality of God's love to them. The children are presented, their names are inscribed, the role of the godparents is recognized and the elect are dismissed after the intercession and final prayer.

The Penitential Rites (Scrutinies)   The penitential rites (scrutinies) are described as major occasions in the catechumenate and are held within a celebration of the word of God as a "kind of scrutiny." The guidelines for the scrutinies in the adult rite are to be followed and adapted for the penitential rites for children, since they have a similar purpose. The children's rites differ from the adult rites, which are primarily designed for the elect, in that they are to be for the benefit of all who will participate—catechumens, parents, godparents and the "baptized companions from the catechetical group." Moreover, there is a curious note in the description of these scrutinies. The text says that these penitential rites are a proper occasion for the baptized children to celebrate the sacrament of penance for the first time. At least one penitential rite is to be celebrated, and if it is convenient, a second one should be arranged. The laying on of hands is offered as an option to the anointing with oil within the penitential rites. The anointing with the oil of catechumens is now reserved to the period of the catechumenate and the period of purification and enlightenment. It is ordinarily deleted from the preparation rites on Holy Saturday or in the celebration of initiation at the Easter Vigil or at another time (#33.7).[8]

The Celebration of the Sacraments of Initiation. In the celebration of the sacraments of initiation, it is customary for the child to be confirmed after baptism, unless there is some extraordinary circumstance. The rite clearly intends that confirmation follow baptism and precede eucharist. The rite of initiation is followed by a period of *mystagogia* that is provided to assist the young neophytes and their companions who have completed their Christian initiation. "This period can be arranged by an adaptation of the guidelines given for adults" (#330).

THE ROLE OF THE COMMUNITY

The children's progress in formation will depend on the help and example of their parents and other adults as well as their friends and classmates (#254). The support and participation of a community is a recurring theme throughout the text on the children's catechumenate. The children's formation should take place within a group in order that the child might experience the life of a Christian community. The introduction notes that since the children to be initiated already belong to a group of children of the same age who are already baptized and are now preparing for confirmation and the eucharist, their Christian initiation should take place gradually and within the supportive context of this group (#254.1). This same instruction is repeated in #256, which states that the candidates should come to the sacraments of initiation at the same time that their baptized companions are to receive confirmation or the eucharist.

The text is not entirely clear on the identity of these "baptized companions" or on the meaning of "catechetical age," but the statement may reflect the situation of the European church at the time that the rite was written. In the early 1970s in many countries throughout Europe, children were ordinarily baptized as infants and generally received confirmation and eucharist at the age of seven or eight years old.[9] Moreover, since the *Code of Canon Law* (canon 891) makes "about the age of discretion" the norm for the age of confirmation, and the revision of the *Rite of Confirmation* states that "confirmation is generally postponed until about the seventh year," it would seem that these "baptized companions" are assumed to be the child's peer group of about the age of seven or eight years old.

The make-up of the "group of companions" has a number of possibilities. They may be the peer group of the child's school class or religious education group; they could be cousins or a family grouping, or most likely they could be baptized but uncatechized children who seek to complete their Christian initiation. The text does not address the question of those children baptized as Christians of other traditions or baptized but uncatechized children of the Roman Catholic tradition. The similarity of the penitential rites for children and the optional penitential rites for baptized but uncatechized adults would seem to indicate that these "baptized companions" are uncatechized children. However, the word "candidate," which in the rite for adults designates those baptized in another tradition, seems in this text to be used for the unbaptized.

Whoever the baptized companions may be, the concern here is that there is a group with whom the child can share faith. The presence of a supportive community is especially important for the celebration of the rites. The text suggests that children who are catechumens should be grouped together for the liturgical celebrations (#255) and representatives of the local community—parents, family, classmates and some adult friends—should also participate. The text cautions against having too large a group present lest the children are made uncomfortable and self-conscious (#256 and 260).

The role of the adult community in the formation of the child is assumed, and the text simply says that children should receive as much help and example as possible from the parents, whose permission is required for the children to be initiated. The period of initiation also provides a good opportunity for the family to have contact with priests and catechists (#254.2). This last statement is as close as the introduction comes to the question of a catechesis for parents. Some parishes that have implemented the children's catechumenate have generally found it effective in direct proportion to the involvement and support of the parents or guardians.[10] It is important to interview the parents or guardians at the beginning of the precatechumenate in order to get some idea of the background from which the child comes, to determine the measure of the degree of support the child can expect and whether or not the parents are willing to participate in some catechetical instruction for themselves.

The parents need to understand the purpose and meaning of the catechumenate so that they perceive the process as a positive value and not a sanction or punishment of some kind. Most of all, these parents need a sense of welcome and a setting characterized by openness in order that they can work through their own relationship to the church. If the parent gives permission for the child's initiation but is not willing to enter into the process, then the catechist should carefully explain the role of the sponsor and of the godparent. The order for children specifies that if parents cannot be present at the rites, their place should be taken by sponsors (#260).[11] In the RCIA, the catechumen has a sponsor, the person who accompanies the candidate seeking admission to the catechumenate. The godparent, who may or may not have been the sponsor, with the approval of the priest, represents the local Christian community from the time of the catechumen's election and testifies to the community about the individual. In the children's order, the sponsor is only present as an alternative to the parent, but the ministry of godparent is included. This inconsistency between the RCIA and the accommodation for children may be explained in part by the fact that children of catechetical age are in a special category. For the purposes of Christian initiation they are considered adults (canon 852.1) on the one hand, but on the other hand, at this stage of their lives they cannot be treated as adults because they are still dependent upon their parents or guardians. Therefore, the parent has the primary responsibility for walking with the child in the journey of faith. If the parents do not accept the responsibility, a sponsor may act in their place. In actual practice, it would seem well for the child to have a sponsor also, perhaps as much for the benefit of the parent as for the child.

ADAPTATION

Episcopal conferences may adapt and add to the rite in order to meet local needs (#258). In November of 1986, the conference of bishops of the United States added several rites—the rite of election for children, for example—for specific groups and circumstances in this country.[12] The instructions and prayers have been adapted to the understanding of the children and the rites for the presentation of the Creed and the Lord's Prayer may be adapted and incorporated into the rite for children.

In following this form of the rite, the celebrant is encouraged to use the options provided freely and wisely (#259), particularly in the special circumstances outlined in *Christian Initiation,* General Introduction, #34–35; in the *Rite of Baptism for Children,* #31; and in the *Rite of Christian Initiation of Adults,* Introduction, #35. The RCIA provides the principles for all accommodations to children.

IMPLICATIONS FOR SACRAMENTAL PRACTICE

The children's form of the RCIA raises some serious questions for catechesis and sacramental initiation since it highlights many inconsistencies in our current practice. Perhaps the most puzzling aspect of the order for children is the assertion that the penitential rites are "a proper occasion for baptized children of the catechetical group to celebrate the sacrament of penance for the first time" (#293).[13]

This statement raises several questions. Whose rite is this? The insertion of the sacrament of penance into the lenten rites of the catechumenate seriously compromises and confuses the status of the catechumen. While the celebrations are certainly of benefit to all who participate, in the RCIA they primarily are intended as a means of conversion for the catechumen. What is the purpose of these rites? The text (#192) describes them as a "kind of scrutiny" that is to be patterned on the guidelines given for the scrutinies for the adult rite. The RCIA (#141) claims that the scrutinies are rites for self-searching and repentance. They are meant to uncover all that is weak and sinful in the hearts of the elect so that they might be healed and be freed from the power of sin, protected from temptation and strengthened in Christ who is the way, the truth, and the life. The rite of penance is a renewal of baptism and a sign of reconciliation. The insertion of the sacrament of penance into the initiation process is a glaring example of the ambiguities of current sacramental practice.

The problem seems to arise because of the ambiguity described earlier about those who are the "baptized companions from the catechetical group." The introduction to the children's catechumenate makes no mention of children who were baptized as infants but are uncatechized or of children baptized in other Christian traditions who are now asking full membership in the Roman Catholic tradition. If these are the children who are the "companions from the catechetical group," then there is somewhat of a parallel with the RCIA, which states that "during the lenten season penitential services should be arranged in such a way as to prepare the baptized but uncatechized for the sacrament of penance" (#408). The RCIA, however, does not stipulate that baptized adults are to celebrate the sacrament, but simply indicates that the celebrations are to prepare for the sacrament. Moreover, this penitential celebration is to be kept separate and distinct from the scrutinies of the elect since the prayer of exorcism "properly belongs to the elect and contains many images referring to their approaching baptism" (#463). To combine the scrutinies and the sacramental celebration distorts and diminishes both rites.

In and of itself, this penitential rite has positive value for the baptized because it highlights several foundational principles of catechesis for the sacrament of reconciliation.[14] The celebration of the sacrament of reconciliation is "a serious striving to perfect the grace of baptism so that, as we bear in our body the death of Jesus Christ, his life may be seen in us ever more clearly" (*Rite of Penance,* 7b). The nature of penance as a renewal of baptism becomes more evident in the context of the lenten season. The liturgical rites underline the ecclesial dimension of the sacrament and through the proclamation of the word and the shared ritual, clarify that the celebration of the sacrament is ecclesial worship. These positive values are all the more reason why the norms of the RCIA should be followed and the penitential rite should "be kept separate and distinct" (#463) from the scrutinies.

SACRAMENT OF CONFIRMATION

With regard to the celebration of the sacraments of initiation, the accommodation of the RCIA to children again contains some ambiguity. The text states that the celebration of the sacraments of initiation should preferably take place at the Easter vigil or on a Sunday. "But the provisions of #256 should also be considered in determining when to celebrate the sacraments of initiation" (#304). When we turn back to the now familiar #256, we find the statement:

> Celebration [of the sacraments of initiation] must also be consistent with the program of catechetical instruction they are receiving, since the candidates should, if possible, come to the sacraments of initiation at the time that their baptized companions are to receive confirmation or eucharist.

In contrast to #256, #305 states that

> At this third step of their Christian initiation, the children will receive the sacrament of baptism, the bishop or priest who baptizes them will also confer confirmation, and the children will for the first time participate in the liturgy of the eucharist.

Moreover, #308 states that baptized children of the catechetical group may be completing their Christian initiation in the sacrament of confirmation and the eucharist at this same celebration. Paragraph 329 reminds the presider to give special attention to any previously baptized children of the catechetical group who at this celebration are to receive communion for the first time.

The National Statutes for the Catechumenate,[15] approved by the National Conference of Catholic Bishops in 1986, mandates that adult candidates, including children of catechetical age, are to receive baptism, confirmation and eucharist in a single eucharistic celebration, whether at the Easter vigil, or if necessary, at some other time (#14, following canon 842.2). Statute 18 repeats the same directive, and #19 is even clearer when it says that some of the ordinary catechetical instruction of baptized children before their reception of the sacraments of confirmation and eucharist may appropriately be shared with catechumens of catechetical age. "Their condition and status as catechumens, however, should not be compromised or confused, nor should they receive the sacraments of initiation in any sequence other than that determined in the ritual of Christian initiation."

The bottom line is that the catechumen of catechetical age is to be confirmed following baptism and preceding eucharist.[16] In the United States, which has such a wide diversity in the age of confirmation, it might seem that confirmation at seven is simply one more option. But these documents, in maintaining the unity of the sacraments of initiation, seem to indicate that something more than age is being considered here.

When one reads the documents cumulatively—the RCIA (#34) and its accommodation to children of catechetical age, the *Rite of Confirmation* (#13), the *Code of Canon Law* (canon

885) and the National Statutes for the Catechumenate—a clear pattern begins to form, namely, that confirmation should precede eucharist for all children, even those baptized as infants. Perhaps the phoenix that is now rising from the ashes will be a consistent sacramental practice with regard to the sacraments of initiation. Some parishes and areas of the country are already "experimenting" with the restoration of the sequence of the sacraments of initiation and implementing the practice of confirmation and eucharist at about the age of seven.[17] This practice has a number of catechetical implications, and we need to draw upon the experience of these parishes. Currently, we have a variety of practices and no clear sense of direction.

CATECHESIS

"The Message to the People of God" of the 1977 Synod of Bishops on Catechesis in our Time[18] calls the catechumenate "the model" for all catechesis, and the National Catechetical Directory, *Sharing the Light of Faith,* states that the catechumenate provides a norm for all catechetical as well as liturgical practice with regard to initiation (#115). This does not mean that the catechumenate is to be seen as some sort of educational program, but it does mean that the principles in the introduction to the RCIA are foundational for catechesis and call for a radical rethinking of current practice.

Currently, our catechetical sessions for children are, in general, organized around a doctrinal concept. The lesson is developed by beginning with some aspect of the children's experience that will enable them to understand the concept, drawing upon an appropriate biblical text and culminating with some activity that will integrate the three aspects of experience, scripture and doctrine. Different forms of prayer or service activities are sometimes included but frequently have the purpose of reinforcing the concept.

Catechesis patterned on the catechumenate is to be gradual and complete, adapted to the liturgical year, solidly supported by celebrations of the word in order to lead catechumens not only to "an appropriate acquaintance with dogmas and precepts but also to a profound sense of the mystery of salvation" (#75.1). All catechetical instruction is to be in the context of prayer (#84). In other words, the catechumenate is liturgical catechesis, and the primary formative experiences for the catechumen are the liturgy, particularly the liturgical rites of the RCIA.

Liturgical catechesis has the task of raising consciousness, of helping the child to become aware of the mystery of salvation, not simply as a past event but as it is manifest in the life of this particular child and this particular community. The child's awareness of the mystery will not come about by explanation but by experience. The awareness will not be fostered by speaking about the liturgy but by letting the language and the ritual of the liturgy speak for itself. The proclamation of the word is a communal activity that most often evokes an affective response in children because the child recognizes something of his or her own feelings or experience in the story. The images challenge, accumulate and coalesce. The shared story is a starting point for awareness that gradually becomes a new vision. The prayers of the liturgical season, the rites that are celebrated and the symbols that store meaning are all part of the formative process. The liturgical rites that mark the steps of the journey and all of the rites—presentation of the cross, celebrations of the word of God, minor exorcisms, blessings and anointing of the catechumens, presentations and scrutinies—that belong to the periods of the catechumenate are a catechesis that speaks to the imagination and memory and that opens the way for the child to enter into the mystery that is God.

The order of initiation for children of catechetical age contains several ambiguous and inconsistent elements within the text that need to be addressed. The way in which it is implemented will need to rely closely on the norms of the RCIA. Nevertheless, this does not diminish the fact that the catechumenate for children is a powerful way of initiating children into the Christian community, one that can enable them to enter into relationship with the living God, share in the community's life of faith and establish a sense of belonging and identity as Christians. The implementation of the children's catechumenate will present many challenges, but perhaps the most significant task that lies ahead is how to bring existing catechetical programs and sacramental practice into a unified, organic process that characterizes the Christian life as an ongoing journey of conversion.

Endnotes

1. Ronald Lewinski, 'Toward a Children's Catechumenate," in *Christian Initiation Resources Reader,* vol. 4 (New York: W. H. Sadlier, 1984) 100–11, describes three general categories of children: those whose parents are catechumens, children of nonpracticing parents and children enrolled in Catholic schools who themselves ask for baptism.

2. A helpful discussion on the text of the children's catechumenate is F. C. Sokol, "Evaluating the Rites for Children," *Liturgy 4* (Winter 1983): 87–91.

3. In 1974, a first, or provisional ("green book") translation of the *Rite of Christian Initiation of Adults* (issued with a brown cover!), published by the United States Catholic Conference, was made available for use in parishes of the United States. The final edition of this text, the "white book," was published by International Commission on English in the Liturgy (ICEL) in January 1986. In November of 1986, the National Conference of Catholic Bishops of the United States approved the "white book," added a series of adaptations for the RCIA in the United States, a list of National Statutes and a five-year plan for implementation. This edition was confirmed by the Holy See on February 19, 1988.

4. For an insightful critique of the Rite of Acceptance, see R. Fragomeni, "Acceptance into the Order of Catechumens," *Catechumenate* 9 (January 1987): 2–11.

5. The adaptation of the rite of children used in France, *Ritual du bapteme des enfants en age de scolarité* (Chalet-Tardy, 1977) provides a ceremony for welcome at the beginning of the precatechumenate that stresses the community dimension of initiation. The assembly gathers to witness the child's request for baptism and the consent of the parents. The priest gives a short exhortation, reminding the children that they are not alone in their journey of faith and asks the community to designate their support by joining hands with the child and with one another. The priest then says a closing prayer that again

underlines the responsibility of the community in fostering the faith of the child.

6. In accord with the Latin text, the children's order names the penitential rites as the second step. Since the United States Bishops' Conference has now added a rite of election for children, it would be a better correspondence with the RCIA to name the rite of election the second step and the penitential rites (scrutinies) as rites belonging to the period of enlightenment.

7. Paragraph 281, following the instruction of the *Directory for Masses with Children* (#24), permits one of the adults to speak to the children after the gospel if the priest finds it difficult to adapt the homily to the language and understanding of the children.

8. See G. Austin, "Anointing with the Oil of Catechumens," *Catechumenate* 9 (September 1987): 2–10.

9. For the current situation on the age for confirmation in France, see O. Sarda, "La confirmation: Les pratiques actuelles en France," *La Maison Dieu* 168 (1986): 117–42, whose study of the French diocesan bulletins published between 1973 and 1986 shows that the general tendency is to delay the age of confirmation.

There is a great diversity in the dioceses of France with regard to age. In 1975–1976, the age for confirmation was about 11 to 13 years old, but the current practice is to confirm about the age of 13 to 15 years. Another interesting study, "Naissances, baptemes et participation au catechisme" is done by J. Potel and O. Sarda in *La Maison Dieu* 152 (1982): 37–100, that reports on several European countries where the practice of infant baptism has decreased and the number of unbaptized children who enroll in catechetical programs has increased.

10. See A. B. Henderson, "Approaches to the Catechumenate for School-age Children and Youth," *Catechist* 17 (September 1983): 24–25.

11. On the question of sponsors, see C. Brusselmans, "From RCIC to RCIA Back to RCIC: The Christian Initiation of Children,"

Forum: North American Forum on the Catechumenate 3 (Fall 1986): 3–4.

12. An overview of these additions is given by R. Lewinski, "The Bishops and the RCIA in Washington: November 1986," *Catechumenate* 9 (January 1987): 15–19.

13. The form of the rite for children in France does not include the sacrament of penance as part of these penitential rites.

14. J. Lopresti presents cogent arguments against the practice of preparing candidates for confession before the Easter Vigil celebration of their initiation. See "Scrutinies or Confession?" *Catechumenate* 9 (March 1987): 15–19.

15. See appendix three of the approved ritual edition of the *Rite of Christian Initiation of Adults* for the Dioceses of the United States of America.

16. It is the opinion of canonist J. Huels that "for those baptized according to the RCIA, namely those who are seven years old or older and have the use of reason, all three sacraments *must* be given at the same celebration." See *The Age of Confirmation: A Canonist's View," Catechumenate* 9 (November 1987): 34.

17. See T. McKenzie and M. Savalesky, "Confirmation with first Communion: It Works!" *Chicago Catechumenate* 8 (May 1986): 16–23; R. P. Moudry, "The Initiation of Children: The Path One Parish Took, *Catechumenate* 9 (July 1987): 27–33; for a canonical basis for the practice, see M. J. Balhoff, "Age for Confirmation: Canonical Evidence," *The Jurist* 45 (1985): 549–587; J. Huels in note no. 16.

18. *The Living Light* 15 (Spring 1978): 91.

Unbaptized Children: A Parish Challenge

RICHELLE PEARL-KOLLER

More and more frequently, people joining parishes today are doing so after a period of separation from the Catholic church. Sometimes this separation is due to real alienation from the church. More often, however, it comes after a period of drifting away from organized religion in general. While the drift away from church upsets parents and grandparents, this is a normal and natural part of coming into adulthood for many people. Furthermore, in most of these situations, while people discontinue regular attendance at church, they do not drop their faith and belief in God. Many still pray regularly and strive to live according to the Christian values they learned in their homes. In no way should separation from the institutional church be seen as synonymous with a separation from God.

But then some event occurs that leads these people to reexamine the church question. Usually it is not a dramatic event that starts this reassessment. It might be a thirtieth birthday, an invitation from a friend to come to church, or a gnawing awareness that something is missing in their life. It might possibly be a death. Any of these could be the trigger that initiates the journey back to regular worship and participation in church.

OUT OF STEP

When these persons come to join the parish they often feel embarrassed and out of step because not only have they been away from the church, they may also have children who were never baptized as infants.

That's the story, for example, of George and Carol and their daughters, seven-year-old Jennifer and nine-year-old Sara. George and Carol have been away from the church since college. When the children were born they decided not to have them baptized so that, as Carol said, "they could choose their own religion when they grew up." But then the neighbors, who were Catholic, lost a child in an auto accident. George and Carol were touched by the way those parents dealt with their tragedy. It was obvious that faith and their church helped them navigate their pain and come up standing on their feet. Carol and George realized something was missing in their own lives. They also realized that something was missing for their children. So they came to the parish asking, "Could we have our children baptized?"

PASTORAL RESPONSE

How would your parish deal with this "out-of-sync" family? What is your parish posture and response? To make them feel guilty? To recognize that leaving the church may be part of maturing? To heal where healing is necessary? To say we're sorry, where that is appropriate? Do you put families like this through more ecclesiastical hoops or tell them to wait until next fall? Or do you say, "Come, let's sit down and talk. Let's share our stories"?

BEGIN WITH A VISION

These are the kinds of families we are talking about when we talk about unbaptized children and catechumenal ministry. In order to know how to minister to these children and their families, we need to situate their stories within the broader context of the church's ministry of initiation. Catechumenal ministry with unbaptized children begins first and foremost with an understanding of the church's vision of initiation. So first we need to identify a few key elements of that vision.

WHAT IT IS, WHAT IT ISN'T

When we talk about initiation we are not talking about another program for children in the church. No, we are talking about the sacraments of the church. We are talking about liturgy, rituals and worship, not programs and lesson plans. Basically we are talking about the church's order of initiation, which is contained in the *Rite of Christian Initiation of Adults*. Everything that we do to initiate children must flow out of this vision of initiation.

We always need to remember that there is only one rite of Christian initiation, the *Rite of Christian Initiation of Adults*. This rite has several adaptations, which are given in part II of the ritual. It is there that we find the directions for what we are to do with unbaptized children of catechetical age. We should never work with the rite's adaptation for children, however, without seeing this adaptation in its whole context as a part of the adult rite. The adult rite is normative for initiation: It sets the direction, the tone for all the adaptations.

IMPLICATIONS

When working with unbaptized children, each section of the rite must be read in light of two questions:

> 1. What vision and direction does the church give us for this period in the adult rite?
>
> 2. How does that direction and vision apply to this adaptation for children?

This is what I would term *contextual reading of the rite.* What we do with children is always done in light of what we do with adults. One obvious and very practical implication of this principle is that in a parish there would never be two catechumenal teams: one for adults, one for children. The parish should have only one catechumenal team where different people carry out the various catechumenal ministries, one of which is to work with unbaptized children of catechetical age.

The church's vision of initiation reminds us, however, that when dealing with unbaptized children of catechetical age we do not put them in "the children's catechumenate." For in this vision of initiation there is no such thing as "a catechumenate," nor is there a "children's catechumenate." To speak of the catechumenate suggests that somewhere, out there, perhaps in our church, our school, our parish center, this object, "the catechumenate," exists. Thinking of a preexistent institution called "catechumenate" is completely contrary to the church's vision and understanding of initiation. No, the catechumenate does not exist. There are only people seeking membership in the church. We call these people *catechumens,* for after the rite of acceptance they enter into one of the orders of the church, the order of catechumens.

NO PREPACKAGED PROGRAMS

In the church, an *order* is a group of people. The "order of catechumens" refers to those persons who have experienced an initial conversion to Christ and are preparing for baptism. There is only one order of catechumens and it is made up of all persons seeking baptism, be they four, fourteen, forty or eighty years old. Ministry to this order, to this group of people, is called *catechumenal ministry.* Catechumenal ministry is changed and shaped by the individuals who seek to join the church. No preexistent, packaged programs are possible with this vision. Catechumenal ministry to the unbaptized child begins with that child and that child's family.

SO, WHERE DO WE START?

By now you're probably saying, though, "That's all fine, but what do I do with Jennifer and Sara? Where do I begin in working with them?"

The place to begin is with their parents. Catechumenal ministry to unbaptized children begins with the family. We need to be sure the parents know they are not alone, nor are they "bad" because they did not have their children baptized as infants. The most pressing issue for them in returning to the church shouldn't be the rush to have the children baptized. Rather, the church urges them to take all the time necessary for themselves as adults to reenter and become regular worshipers in the Sunday assembly. Just as we do with infant baptism, the church looks for the faith of the parents. Efforts must be made to connect family with family and to mainstream people into the life of the parish.

Why the delay? Why the emphasis on the parents and the family, when it is the child who will be baptized? For all practical purposes, the child is entering into the change that is occurring in his or her own family. Psychologists estimate that agencies such as school and church can match no more than one-tenth of the parents' influence when it comes to forming the values and attitudes of children. Parents, whether they know it or not, are the key formers of their children's religious values, beliefs and attitudes. It is in watching the parents worship, pray and try to live by the gospel that a child comes to understand what it means to be a believer. Faith for everyone, but especially for a child, is more caught than taught. This is why, at first, our catechumenal ministry needs to focus more directly on the parents and family system than on the child.

PRACTICAL APPROACH

Still, I hear you saying "Give me something practical! What do we do in our parish with these children?" I cannot give you a recipe card because in catechumenal ministry, "nothing can be determined a priori" (RCIA, 76). Mess, flexibility and adaptation are the name of the game. Every catechumenal ministry is individualized. There is no set program.

Along with the vision sketched above, however, there are eight principles that can be used to guide a parish as it begins working with unbaptized children of catechetical age:

> 1. Catechumenal ministry with children follows the same ritual and steps as catechumenal ministry with adults, but all is adapted to the child.

> 2. The rites set the agenda for what happens during each stage of catechumenal ministry. The rites act as bridges directing what should happen in the period before and after the rite.

> 3. Initiation of children takes place primarily in the midst of the Sunday assembly.

> 4. The only way for unbaptized children of catechetical age to enter the church is through full initiation. That is, baptism, confirmation and eucharist are received together, in that order, at one ceremony, the Easter Vigil.

> 5. Children's formation is done with companions, peers, family and other members of the community.

> 6. There is no set length of time for the initiation of children. Their initiation may be extended over several years if need be (RCIA, 253).

> 7. Liturgy and catechesis are wed in this rite (RCIA, 75), so that catechumenal activities with children are more ritual and liturgy centered than education and school centered.

> 8. The goal of initiation is to bring children to the eucharist and from there to lead them to mission in the world.

Carefully probed, each of these principles will enable a parish to design a ministry faithful to the church vision of initiation and responsive to the needs of the growing number of unbaptized older children in our parishes. And in all this we are guided by Jesus' words: "Let the little children come to me."

Unbaptized Children: What Can We Do?

DON NEUMANN

There are growing numbers of children in our parishes who have never been baptized. Whether that is due to the inactive faith of their parents at the time of the birth of the child or to other extenuating factors, the children are here, and their numbers are increasing.

In the past these children have been termed "special cases." Sometimes they were called "out-of-sequence" cases, because they did not follow the usual pattern of reception of baptism at infancy, first communion at or near age seven, and confirmation at or near the age of 12 or high school (or whenever the parish deems it appropriate). They have been inserted into existing parochial religious education programs, with or without much attention to their unique backgrounds or needs. In many cases, they have been unintentionally treated as "stepchildren," or exceptions to the norm because their numbers are still smaller than those who follow the custom we have adopted regarding sacramental celebrations of infant baptism, first communion and confirmation.

But these children are exceptions and misfits no longer. In February 1988, Rome gave the approval for the English translation of the *Rite of Christian Initiation of Adults,* with the specific American adaptations approved by the bishops of the United States in November 1986. Within this rite for adults is a rite for "Christian Initiation for Children Who Have Reached Catechetical Age." The conscientious implementation of this rite of initiation of children of a catechetical age could seriously alter all the presuppositions we have had thus far about what is norm and what is custom.

As the rite states, it is intended for children who have attained the use of reason, and are thereby at a "catechetical age." They come to the process either under parental influence or on their own initiative. While the rite is very explicit regarding the importance of parents, family and peers in the process, the focus of the rite is upon children who are able to be catechized.

Traditionally, we have understood the age of reason to be at or near seven years. Today, however, with the contemporary studies in learning patterns of infants and young toddlers, some education specialists might well challenge seven years as the earliest age at which children begin to learn. Some specialists say that learning begins as early as a few months after birth (or even from within the womb). Children who are able to be catechized, therefore, could probably be five years of age, or in some cases, even younger.

Regardless of how the specialists tackle the "catechetical age" questions, the rite for the initiation of children of a catechetical age addresses some very specific situations in which many of our parishioners find themselves, and it sets forth some very concrete recommendations of how and in what manner the initiation of children should take place.

CONVERSION

The rite quickly sets forth the expectation that conversion is the goal of the catechumenate experience. For children this will mean different things than it might mean for an adult, but the expectation of conversion (personal and developed) in accord with the age and education of the child is still the core issue. The nature and description of conversion for someone who is seven or eight years of age must still be determined by specialists in the field, and we must clearly admit that some scholars and practitioners would even question whether conversion is possible for someone that young. Regardless, time will clarify the debate and the issues we must consider.

Whatever the theorists resolve about conversion in children, the tradition of the church—to be willing to baptize any who come with firm resolve, sincere motives and adequate preparation—stands firm. Children will always be eligible for baptism, whether at age seven or seventeen, if they are sincere, good-intentioned and sufficiently prepared.

THE NEW ISSUE IS "TIMING"

Of particular concern for parishes and parochial catechetical programs will be the stipulation in the newly approved rite that the process of initiation of children should be extended over several years, if needed, in order to afford the children the necessary formation time and catechesis to be adequately prepared. As in the adult rites, the rite for children of a catechetical age encourages that the progress toward full initiation be marked with rituals and ceremonies to emphasize the child's progression into the faith community. With the help of family and companions, the child progresses step by step in the way of being a follower of Jesus.

What this will mean practically for many parishes is still fairly uncertain. The rite urges that these children be "mixed with other children who are preparing for eucharist and confirmation," yet the rite also asserts that the unbaptized children should be formed, at other times, into groups by themselves. The rite also suggests that the initiation rites for these children coincide with the same celebration at which their peers celebrate first communion or confirmation. Then at another place the rite recommends that these initiation rites occur at the Easter Vigil or at a Sunday Mass of the Easter season.

If one followed all those directives it would seem to suggest that children are only initiated at or near the ages of the reception of first communion or the celebration of confirmation. This would mean that there are only two times in a person's childhood when they could celebrate Christian initiation. Likewise, from the rite, either time chosen would (or better, "should") coincide with the Easter Vigil or Easter Season.

The operative theologies here are obvious. There is one, repeat one, celebration of initiation that has primacy in the Roman Catholic Church: a unified celebration of initiation when the candidate (be it adult or child) is washed (baptism), chrismated lavishly (confirmation) and led to the Lord's table for the heavenly feast (eucharist). All other celebrations of first communion and confirmation make complete sense only when they are seen in the light of their "initiation" origins. Therefore, the rite encourages that the initiation of catechetical age children occur near or within the same celebrations at which their peers would share in their initiation as well.

Given this directive, it seems clear that the theological norm the rite is concerned with preserving is the unified celebration of baptism, confirmation and eucharist as vehicles to give meaning to the custom of celebrating first communion at a time other than baptism and to give clarified meaning to the celebration of confirmation when it is given out-of-normal order for whatever reasons. Norm, here, is the preferred way things should be done. Custom is what we have inherited from history.

Likewise, in the rite it is clearly stated that Easter is the prime time for Christian initiation. Therefore, for the universal Catholic church, Easter is the preferential time for all celebrations of baptism, confirmation and eucharist in the parish. (Oh, for the day when the bishop's confirmation schedule is determined by the theology of our worship rather than the tragic pressures that so many bishops feel to "get them all in" before the end of May.)

Pastorally this also means that Lent is not a prime (or even good) time to baptize—not even infants. Lent is the season for baptismal preparation. Therefore, in most parishes there should be no baptisms of any kind during the Lenten season (unless the infant, child or adult is seriously ill or near death). Lent is the season for preparation for initiation. Easter is the season for celebration of initiation.

What we must relearn is the lesson of the ages: If every season is like the Easter season, then there is no reason to celebrate Easter with any uniqueness at all. If every Sunday is like every other Sunday, then there is nothing to differentiate one from the other, and they are all the same, without unique value or distinctive meaning. Lent has its own rhythm. Easter has quite another. We must be able to fast so that the feast can be what it needs to be.

QUESTIONS FOR PARISHES AND CATECHISTS

The issue for parishes and catechetical programs will be timing. Will American religious educators and parish religious education programs be able to shift gears out of a nine-month academic model (patterned after public-school education) in order to provide catechesis (word formation of children) that is based upon a twelve-month liturgical year (Years A, B and C)? Will parishes dare to trust that the Sunday liturgy of the word is meant to be the core spiritual formation of the Catholic faithful and the catechumens (adult and children alike)? Will children who are catechumens be dismissed with the adults after the homily and prayers for them, so that they may "break open" the riches of the word they have just heard in the Sunday assembly? Will they be dismissed (as it is called for in the National Statutes) for twelve consecutive months, Sunday after Sunday, so that "necessary distinctions" can be made between those "in the womb of the church" and those newly born in water and the spirit? Will we dare challenge all the cultural pressures of instant gratification in our time by being willing to design and foster faith formation processes for children (and adults) that are not simply nine months long, but two or three years (or more) if that is needed? The questions that will burst forth from the implementation of the catechumenate for children are multiple, but the fruit they potentially yield for our renewal and reform is most significant.

A MODEL TO DREAM FROM

What form will this process for children actually take in our parishes? It's time to start working out the details. I present here a model to dream from, a place to begin the discussion. I hope you will add the fruit of your own dreams so that together we can give flesh to a rite that holds great promise for our church.

Step One: Initial Contact

The process begins when parents come to the church to ask for baptism for their children, who are, let us say, ages four, six and eight. After an initial interview and assessment of their family religious history and needs, some initial invitations are offered. Would they like to join a group of other families who have children preparing for initiation? The children might also enroll in regular religious education sessions already occurring in the parish. If the children have absolutely no religious training, this enrollment might be postponed for a later time. At the family sessions, trained facilitators lead the participating families in faith formation experiences aimed at producing initial conversion: introduction to God, Jesus and the Spirit; a consciousness of sin and forgiveness; and the church as the community of faith.

How long the children's precatechumenate period should last will depend upon their past religious experience, family support, participation in the life of the parish, and so on. For some it will be three or four months, and for others it may be several months to a year. That is why the role of parents and family is so important. If the support is there, and the interest of the child is sincere, the progression through the various phases should be smooth.

When the children and parents have progressed from "outside" to "hungering to be inside" the family of faith, the rite of acceptance into the order of catechumens is celebrated for the children. This concludes the precatechumenate period and moves the children into the catechumenate phase of preparation for initiation. It is best if the precatechumenate sessions are regularly scheduled so that new inquirers can be received at any time of the year. Such year-round programs are possible if you have an adequate number of team members and resources.

Step Two: The Catechumenate

After the children enter the catechumenate, they begin to attend Mass regularly on Sundays with their families (they may have already been doing this, but now it is essential to the process). After the homily and prayers, the children are dismissed with the adult catechumens to go and "break open" the word of God and the mysteries of faith contained therein. These Sunday-morning catechetical sessions would happen every Sunday of the year and would assist the child to see that the faith of the church and the worship of the church are very tightly interwoven. The goal of all catechesis is the formation of a lifestyle that is consistent with gospel values and behaviors.

In addition to the Sunday morning "breaking open the word" sessions, the children could also continue to take part in the regular religious education sessions that their peers attend (as long as they are ready and capable of taking part in these without unnecessary burden). Peer influence is very important to the catechumenal process. The rite notes this clearly. It also emphasizes the need for peers and companions to give good example to the catechumens who are coming to faith with them. While the rite offers the possibility that the catechumenate might be extended over several years, "if need be," it also seems to imply that the catechumenate should last for at least a few years as a norm. If the catechumenate for children were to last for 36 months, it would provide the children and their families an opportunity to experience the full three-year cycle of scriptures that form our Catholic lectionary. In terms of religious formation, it would provide a relaxed and yet intense encounter with the faith of Christians and the faith of the Catholic Church. It would also provide ample opportunity for the children and their families to become involved in parish life, and become known and nurtured by the community. It would enable them to have numerous opportunities for feeding the hungry, clothing the naked and visiting the sick, all of which are part of the apostolic mission of the faithful.

In three years of catechumenal formation, many aspects of an individual's lifestyle can be directed, and many behaviors can be altered, to become consistent with the gospel. But it takes a willingness to take the time to let it happen. It takes time for the fruits of the Spirit to ripen. Will we dare take this necessary time?

The catechumenate should last long enough to ensure that the necessary program of instruction and formation is complete and that nothing has been abbreviated or short-circuited.

When consistency of faith and openness to the continuing transformation that God is weaving in the fabric of humanity is evidenced in the catechumens, they are thereby ready to be called to the Easter sacraments.

Step Three: Immediate Preparation for Initiation

The lenten period would serve the same function for children that it does for adults: It is the period of purification and enlightenment, a time to prepare ever more closely to be alert to the deceits of evil in our world. Children must have a desire to be initiated into the body of Christ in order to celebrate the rite of election. The church, their families, catechists, sponsors and parish family recognize and call them as the chosen ones of God. During these final 40 days of preparation, their immediate focus will be on their continued need to be open to whatever God calls them, and to trust in God and not merely in themselves.

Celebration of Initiation If the children are old enough, perhaps the Easter Vigil will be the best time to celebrate their Christian Initiation. Pastorally, we have found that those who are in their teen years have a better possibility of entering into the richly complex Vigil of Easter than do seven or eight year olds.

For these younger children, Easter Sunday has proven a prime time of celebration. With their peers present on the great solemnity of Easter, children enter the tomb-font of baptism and are "washed in the life-giving waters." Full immersion or bathing is a rich expression of the lavishness of grace being poured out in this moment. Then standing engulfed in a white towel, they are generously chrismated (confirmed) and invited to the table of the Lord to feast. Only when all three initiation sacraments are generously celebrated can the full power and meaning of our holy faith come forth.

Step Four: Postbaptismal Catechesis, or Mystagogia

Following the format in the adult rite, the postbaptismal catechesis for newly initiated children can be a most dynamic time of celebration and sacramental instruction. Because baptism, confirmation and eucharist are so fresh in the experience of the children, they can share weekly with their peers what they have come to understand about Jesus and the kingdom through their own initiation, and their peers can share what they have come to know about Jesus in their experience of life and faith. It can be a time of celebrations, storytelling about "new birth" experiences and what they mean for us, celebration of eucharist with the Sunday assembly, and making connections with the family of faith to which they have now become most concretely connected. It can also be a time when the children might share their knowledge and experience of Jesus with the whole parish family (after Mass, in home gatherings, etc.) so that the parable of the little children might once again have its impact on the life of the church.

The National Statutes on the Catechumenate also state that newly baptized adults should gather monthly for sharing support and for further instruction until the anniversary of their initiation. The same could be said for newly baptized children of a catechetical age. While they would receive nurturing in the religious education sessions of their peers, they still need the support and nurturing of the smaller, specialized community of faith that brought them to birth.

Significant celebrations should mark the anniversary of the children's initiation. What a church we could be if we all saw Easter as our "birth feast" and the touchstone of our truest selves!

GREAT PROMISE

The catechumenate for children holds some great surprises in store for this grand and glorious church of ours. Most of all it holds the promise that we can have life and have it to the full—if we will only risk the price.

The Rite of Christian Initiation Adapted for Children: First Steps

GAEL GENSLER

The catechumenate is alive and well in your parish. You sit back to breathe a sigh of contentment, "Ah, at last, some routine has returned to my life." Then the phone rings and the caller tells you that some of the catechumens have expressed a desire to have their children initiated into the Catholic church. Or some former parishioners are returning to the practice of their faith and want to have their children baptized. "What next?" Do such requests arise in your parish?

ADULT CATECHUMENATE FIRST

So you want to establish a children's catechumenate—what do you do? In the *Rite of Christian Initiation of Adults* (RCIA), part II, chapter 1, "Christian Initiation of Children Who Have Reached Catechetical Age" is modeled on the adult experience. In RCIA, 253, we read,

> Accordingly, as with adults, [children's] initiation is to be extended over several years, if need be, before they receive the sacraments. Also as with adults, their initiation is marked by several steps. . . . Corresponding to the periods of adult initiation are the periods of the children's catechetical formation that lead up to and follow the steps of their initiation.

Before a parish develops a ministry of Christian initiation of children, a preliminary question must be asked. Is Christian initiation of adults in place in that parish? The RCIA needs to be implemented in a parish before implementation of a children's catechumenate is considered. With that clearly in mind, what other issues need to be addressed concerning the children's catechumenate?

A FAMILY MINISTRY

The initial family interview is key in determining who the real inquirer is and what the family's prior experience of faith has been. "Catechetical age" can mean many things—from age 6 or 7 to age 17 or 18—and catechetical success can hinge on appropriate age groupings.

A checklist for gathering information may include: Who are the families—adults and children—who are approaching initiation? What are the ages of the children? Where do they live? In what school system are they enrolled? What has been their experience with faith? What has been their experience with church? Several things must be acknowledged:

> [Children] seek Christian initiation either at the direction of their parents or guardians or, with parental permission, on their own initiative. Such children are capable of receiving and nurturing a personal faith and of recognizing an obligation in conscience but they cannot yet be treated as adults. At this stage of their lives, they are dependent on their parents or guardians and are still strongly influenced by their companions and their social surroundings." (RCIA, 252)

Another key issue related to the family is sponsorship. "The children's progress in the formation they receive depends on the help and example of their companions and on the influence of their parents" (254). In practice, perhaps a sponsor for a parental catechumen has children of similar ages, and a sponsor's family may be willing to sponsor a catechumen's family. Or catechumenal children may have classmates or friends who are members of the parish, and some of their families may be willing to sponsor the children. It frequently works well to provide family-to-family sponsorship.

CATECHESIS

Another question to consider is, "Who will do this?" The catechumenate and religious education directors need to collaborate to find an answer to this question. Perhaps the parish already has a liturgy of the word for children on Sunday mornings in which the youngest catechumens could participate. These young catechumens could be dismissed from this group to continue their formation based on the lectionary readings. Older catechumens—teens, for example—could be dismissed with the adults and then form their own group for reflection on the word. The catechetical sessions are based on the issues and questions that flow from reflections of the younger and older catechumens on the word, and the topics are suited to the particular age. There may be three groups: ages 7 to 10, 11 to 14 and 15 to 18.

According to RCIA, 255, "It is advantageous, as circumstances allow, to form a group of several children who are in this same situation, in order that by example they may help one another in their progress as catechumens." Of course, no definite groupings can be made without considering the level of development of each of the children. It is possible that some children 16, 17 or 18 years of age might best participate in some or all of the adult sessions.

Children need to be met at whatever level of religious literacy they have reached. To place them in a religious education group that corresponds to their age may place them at a distinct disadvantage if they have little or no formal religious vocabulary or experience. Children need peer support, but that does not necessarily mean they have to be in the same classes as children their own age. Other kinds of support may mean far more.

RITES

What about the celebrations of the various rites? "Rites should be celebrated with the active participation of a congregation that consists of a suitable number of the faithful, the parents, family, members of the catechetical group and a few adult friends" (257).

In some parishes that have implemented the catechumenate adapted for children, children participate in the same liturgical celebrations as the adults, especially if a parent or both parents are catechumens. Whenever possible, the whole family needs to be involved as a family unit—even extended families, if time and distance permit.

How long will it take? It takes as long as it takes! That sounds familiar, but it may also offer some comfort. God's work does not always fit into neat packages and schedules.

So when do you begin? When the parents approach you concerning their children. When are the children initiated? When the parents, the children and members of the team discern their readiness to move onto the next period leading to full initiation at the Easter Vigil.

> The Christian initiation of these children requires both a conversion that is personal and somewhat developed, in proportion to their age, and the assistance of the education they need. The process of initiation thus must be adapted both to their spiritual progress, that is, to the children's growth in faith, and to the catechetical instruction they receive. (253)

Of special consideration is the age of the child. The older the child, the more independent her or his role will be in the whole process, especially the responsibility of discerning readiness for each of the rites. For teenagers, peer support will be of greater importance than for younger children. A good source for sponsors for teens may be young adults in the parish. Closer in age and interests to the teens, they may be more compatible as companions and guides.

What is the role of the Catholic school or the religious education program in the parish? Certainly, the class as a group could act as a sponsor for catechumens of the same age. The class could be present at the celebrations of the rites and social events. They could also write notes or make cards to show their support of the catechumens. Each class could adopt a family. The children who are being initiated could gradually be introduced to their age group in the parish over a period of time and in varied settings.

> Since the children to be initiated often belong to a group of children of the same age who are already baptized and are preparing for confirmation and eucharist, their initiation progresses gradually and within the supportive setting of this group of companions. (254.1)

Great care must be demonstrated that the children will not be embarrassed by their lack of religious affiliation or knowledge as they are integrated into the appropriate peer group.

So now that there are prospective candidates for such a process, you might gather a few interested adults and perhaps a few older children together to discuss the initial needs. The next item on the agenda is to begin.

Christian Initiation of Children: No Longer a Class or Grade Issue

STEVEN M. ROBICH

Considering the mind of the church as expressed in the *Rite of Christian Initiation of Adults,* what are the best means for providing children of catechetical age with religious formation for the sacraments of initiation, most specifically, first eucharist and confirmation? The purpose of this article is to show the value of the catechumenal process and the need for a paradigmatic shift from the classroom method of sacramental preparation to the catechumenal process for those children of catechetical age who are prepared and brought before the community for full initiation. The need for a paradigmatic shift will be demonstrated by contrasting the characteristics of the classroom method of sacramental preparation with the catechumenal process. This article will focus on three components of the preparation process: structure, companions and catechesis. From the outset it will be important to identify the principal theological and pastoral premises that underpin the need for this shift.

WHY CHANGE?

The first premise is that religious formation must be founded on the word of God, which reveals a God who is love, and on the fundamental makeup of the individual, namely the need to be loved and to love. The recognition of these two realities as mutual lends support to the process of religious formation. This premise sets up conditions for the formation and initiation of the individual. it is also reasonable that religious formation would have at its core the bonding characteristic of love.

The second premise focuses on companions. Candidates are joined by faithful companions and are not alone in their preparation for full initiation that must be understood as a journey of faith, with peers, adults and community.

The third premise centers catechesis in the word of God. It involves listening to the work, praying over it and reflecting upon it alone and in groups.

CATECHUMENAL VERSUS PEDAGOGICAL PARADIGMS

At this moment in the life of the church, children born to Catholic families begin the process of sacramental initiation with infant baptism. When children reach the age of reason, usually around age seven, they are prepared for first penance and first eucharist. By ninth or tenth grade, individuals become fully initiated with the sacrament of confirmation. To extend the administration of the sacraments of initiation over a period of approximately 16 years, although this is the current practice with almost all children of Catholic families in the United States, is no longer the norm. The norm for Christian initiation is the catechumenal process.

The catechumenal process employs a paradigm quite different from the pedagogical paradigm used by most religious educators for sacramental preparation. This in turn then calls for a change in the process of religious formation and the periods and rites that mark this process.

If religious educators make efforts to incorporate the catechumenal process into their classroom paradigm for sacramental preparation, a dilemma will, without a doubt, occur in those settings where religious education is for the most part teacher directed, information oriented and age focused. Such incorporation places the catechumenal process of religious growth and formation into a chronologically ordered and programmatically structured reality—the graded classroom.

The academic classroom design is based on student readiness and teacher skill. This does not fit a catechumenal process that is more suited to individual readiness, personal maturity and group bondedness. Granted, the classroom environment lends itself to a particular type of formation, intellectual and social, but it must work well beyond its means if it is to foster the type of spiritual progress called for by the catechumenate itself. Such progress manifests itself in the individual's capacity for receiving and nurturing a personal faith and of recognizing both private and public obligations of conscience.

The catechumenal process emphasizes personalization, variation, adaptation and community-mindedness. As a result, religious formation can take place in the context of small groups of candidates, companions and the guidance of sponsors. Because of its flexibility in respecting both individual and group needs, the catechumenal process provides more opportunities to touch the faith of the whole community through personal witness, action and involvement. Hence, the process lends itself to the involvement of many community members as their gifts are needed and called forth. Candidates proceed through the preparation process gradually within a supportive setting of peers older and younger, parents, pastoral staff, relatives, friends and community members. The responsibility does not reside predominantly with a classroom teacher and classmates.

Such differences suggest a particular course of action with regard to the implementation of the catechumenal process. This would determine that sacramental preparation for first eucharist and confirmation be structurally separate from graded religious education. This design would enable the process of initiation to be based on spiritual growth, social consciousness and liturgical sense rather than academic mastery or grade achievement. Correspondingly, the ministry of companion or sponsor is not primarily one of teaching but rather one of guiding in a common journey of faith.

METHOD IS THE PROBLEM, NOT CONTENT

It is in the area of catechesis that most opposition to this paradigmatic change will be found. Opposition will not occur because of a content problem; rather, it will occur because of the methodology employed. The real fear is that the process of listening, reflecting, praying and sharing cannot be programmed. That leaves many people uncomfortable.

Currently the common method of religious education uses a textbook or catechism. This methodology presents religious beliefs and truths in the same way any other academic subject is presented—fact by fact and concept by concept. This method is not without its consequence. As Josef Jungmann suggests, what is lacking among the faithful is a holistic understanding of the wonderful message of salvation. He says that there is little ignorance of basic Christian doctrine—the sacraments, Christ, Mary, Adam and Eve, God and the church. But what Christians retain of doctrine is a string of dogmas, moral precepts, threats, promises, customs, rites and duties. The textbook and catechism—grade by grade, chapter by chapter, page by page—present Christian truths like links in a chain, "from me to God." Christian truths need to be grouped instead around the center from which they receive their light, like spokes in a wheel. For the Christian, that center can only be Jesus Christ.

LECTIONARY-BASED CATECHESIS

Because the catechumenal process is rooted in the paschal mystery of Jesus Christ, it is closely connected to the church's cycle of Sunday celebrations. What this connection guides us to is lectionary-based catechesis. Lectionary-based catechesis provides the opportunity for individuals to study and "break open" the meaning of the great stories of salvation. With a focus on the gospels especially, individuals gain a greater understanding of what the Christian life demands and who Jesus calls each of us to be. Lectionary-based catechesis as it increases a working knowledge of the sacred texts will also enrich participation at the Sunday celebration. Hence a study of the scriptural tradition through listening to the word, reflecting upon it and praying over it together is a study that hands on beliefs in a living tradition, experienced in the word of God and connection to the Sunday celebration.

For those who may be hesitant about this methodology, it is important to keep in mind that lectionary-based catechesis raises issues of doctrine that are significant to Catholic tradition and that maintain their connection to their source in Jesus Christ. These issues are raised through the agenda set by the cycle of readings, the interest of the group and the personal readiness of the individual children. Therefore, catechesis based on the lectionary cycles can help candidates receive nourishment in faith by the word of God.

In conclusion, the shift from the classroom model to the catechumenal process is necessary if the RCIA is to be successfully implemented. The shift calls for a change in practice: that sacramental preparation be structurally separate from graded religious education, that a broader responsibility be extended across the faith community for faith formation, and that catechesis be based on the lectionary.

Lastly, the catechumenate respects and supports the religious experience as a fundamental experience of love, essential for all human beings. People generally are not satisfied with merely living, but we live in search of love: of being loved and loving. Recalling the words of Rudolf Bultmann, the religious act tends toward a "completion of being." Such striving develops a connaturality between the love-seeker and the God who is love. Hence, religious formation is more than the dissemination of facts or information. Religious formation is a journey of faith, a companion-based process. It is an experience of love, hospitality and welcome. These provide the opportunity for faith to be shared and for the love of God to be named in human life.

Children, Scrutinies and Penitential Rites

RICHELLE PEARL-KOLLER

In the process described for catechumenal ministry with children, the *Rite of Christian Initiation of Adults* calls for the celebration of at least one penitential rite. Paragraph 291 defines this penitential rite "as a kind of scrutiny, similar to the scrutinies in the adult rite. Thus the guidelines given for the adult rite (141–146) may be followed since the children's penitential rites have a similar purpose." Further, the rite states,

> These penitential rites are proper occasions for baptized children of the catechetical group to celebrate the sacrament of penance for the first time. When this is the case, care should be taken to include explanations, prayers and ritual acts that relate to the celebration of the sacrament with these children. (RCIA, 293).

Now this is confusing—a scrutiny, a penitential rite and first confession are all combined and mixed up in one ritual. What is going on here? To sort out this confusion, we must read this portion of the children's adaptation in the context of what is said about the scrutiny in the adult rite. Contextual reading of the rite provides the insight, principles and direction needed to deal with the scrutiny/penitential-rite dilemma.

The scrutiny is a radical confrontation between two worlds: the kingdom of God and the kingdom of evil, the kingdom of darkness and the kingdom of light. Scrutinies are a cry for deliverance from the power of sin and evil, and they are a profession of hope and belief in a God who has triumphed and who continues to triumph over evil. The scrutinies are not so much about personal sin as they are about cosmic evil and its power. In the scrutiny the church cries out *"Kyrie!"* Not "Lord have mercy, *mea culpa*," but "*Kyrie!* Lord! Be ruler! Be Lord here in our midst. Triumph, Jesus Christ, over the power of sin and darkness. Exercise your lordship, your *kyrie!* Here! Now!" This is the understanding of scrutiny in the adult rite:

> The scrutinies are meant to uncover, then heal all that is weak, defective or sinful in the hearts of the elect; to bring out, then strengthen all that is upright, strong and good. For the scrutinies are celebrated in order to deliver the elect from the power of sin and Satan, to protect them against temptation, give them strength in Christ and uncover and heal what is sinful. (141)

SCRUTINIES AND CHILDREN

When it comes to the adaptation of the rites for children, there is a tremendous watering down of this understanding. Unbaptized children coming for initiation are mixed with baptized children coming for first confession. In the mix, the rite's vision of sin as systemic and cosmic evil is trivialized and equated with naughtiness and childhood transgressions. To understand sin in this way is to miss completely the point of the exorcism and scrutiny.

So we ask the question: Do exorcism and scrutiny have a place in the initiation of children? The church certainly thinks so when it initiates infants: There is an exorcism in the *Rite of Infant Baptism*. Why then this difference for children of catechetical age? Are not these children also caught in the confrontation of the two kingdoms?

CHILDREN: VICTIMS OF EVIL

When it comes to evil in the world, children, unlike adults, who are both victims and victimizers of evil, more often are victimized by the evil that exists in the world. Consider some of the risks children face as they encounter evil in our world.

Poverty   One in four children in the United States is poor. One in six children has no health-insurance coverage and so goes without adequate medical care. Many of these same children had minimal or no prenatal care and are low-birthweight children. Physically underdeveloped at birth, many never catch up. Twenty-one percent of our nation's minors live in households with incomes below the poverty level. Fifteen percent of these households are headed by a person working full-time all year at a minimum wage. Forty-thousand children die every day for want of food, clothing, shelter or medical care. Many children have no immunization and so often face a lifetime of poor health. These children are victimized by the inequities of our socioeconomic system. They are caught in a cycle of poverty, a cycle that breeds hopelessness in its victims, who cannot break out. Certainly the power of evil affects our children.

Consumerism   On the other side of the poverty cycle are the children of affluence who are being taught by our system to measure their self-worth by a financial yardstick: "I am what I have or what my parents make." What will happen to these children as they grow up and cannot maintain or match the lifestyle they grew up in? Many children raised in affluence have never known limits, yet limits are part of life. These children are victimized by our consumerism.

Corporate Values   What of the hurried children, who are so programmed, scheduled and stressed out that they have no chance to be children, no opportunity to learn so much by doing nothing? Are they not victims? Children need tolerance, patience and acceptance of chaos if they are to be nurtured and grow. Yet the value system of much of corporate America demands of its executives—these children's parents—workaholism, perfectionism, impatience, restlessness and efficiency for success: values contrary to the needs of children. Again, children are victimized.

Individualism Many children are victimized by American privatism and individualism—my phone, my TV, my room, my, my, my! These children's perception of reality is distorted by a myopic vision that leads to an insular world view. Thus victimized, children are unable to realize that we live and are bound together as humans not in "my world," but in the global village.

War Children who are the victims of the devastating power of war live in dread of violence and terror. Many grow up in our world without hope in the possibility of a future.

TRIUMPH OVER EVIL

Poverty, consumerism, individualism, the values of the corporate world and war are but a few facets of our children's world as it is touched by the power of evil. And what does the Christian community have to say to this? In the rite of scrutiny we say that Jesus Christ has triumphed. We proclaim that life, not evil, triumphs. As members of the Christian community, we stand together against this evil. As Christian believers, we are committed to work to transform the world. We thus become advocates for our children, advocates living in fidelity to the Gospel who strive to change the systems that inflict evil on the innocent.

When children are initiated into this kind of community, they know security. And they know hope. They know that they are bound in a community of solidarity, a community of grownups bound together in Christ, working to change the world and protect them from evil. Just as children in El Salvador or Guatemala grow up knowing that their parents are engaged in activity to change their world, so do our young initiates who take part in a scrutiny learn from the adults what it is to be Christian. They also learn what sin really is. They learn that sin is betraying the cause—to fail to work for justice and mercy so that the kingdom will come.

CHILDREN AND THE RITE OF SCRUTINY

In light of all this, how could we deprive our children of a real scrutiny? How could we substitute a penitential rite and first confession with its peccadillo notion of sin—"I slapped my sister, disobeyed my parents"—for the scrutiny's real notion of sin and its radical proclamation of the gospel, the good news of the saving power of God, *Kyrios,* in our midst?

Examining the hybrid scrutiny-penitential rite for children, we must ask: Do we have two initiatory practices, one for adults and one for children? Do our initiation sacraments and rituals change and have different meanings when they are applied to children? In the rite for the unbaptized adult, there is no mention either of celebrating the sacrament of penance or of bringing baptized persons into the scrutiny for a penitential rite. In fact, the rite makes it clear (461–463) that while a penitential rite may be celebrated for baptized but uncatechized adults, it is to be celebrated apart from and not combined with the scrutiny. The penitential rite is only for the candidates, not for the unbaptized. Further, this rite "may help prepare for the sacrament of penance" (461), but it is not the occasion to celebrate the sacrament. The penitential rite is intended "solely for celebrations with baptized adults preparing for confirmation and eucharist or reception into the full communion of the Catholic Church. . . . The scrutinies for the elect and this penitential rite have been kept separate and distinct" (463).

Why then a shift in practice where children are involved? What prompts the mixing of unbaptized children with baptized children preparing to complete their initiation with confirmation and first communion? What distortions occur in the understanding of a scrutiny when we mix first penance and scrutiny together? Confirmation and eucharist are initiation sacraments. If initiation is the primary celebration of reconciliation, why would the additional celebration of the sacrament of penance be needed for someone who has not yet completed their initiation? These are serious questions that must be borne in mind when examining the children's penitential rite.

Initiation is about entering the community. Reconciliation is about reentry after placing oneself outside the community through serious sin. To join initiation rituals with penitential rites is to blur what is happening in each. In that blurring the power of the scrutiny is lost.

When a real scrutiny, such as that described for adults, is celebrated with children, the whole assembly is challenged to be who they say they are: people of the gospel committed to fight evil and work for the establishment of justice and mercy in our world. Where a real scrutiny is celebrated with children the adult community prays:

> Remember the children, O God,
>> who have no voice
>> to protest the violence and deprivation which,
>> through no fault of theirs,
>> befalls them.
>
> Remember the children in this nation
>> who have no choice
>> about whether they
>> will be healthy and well fed
>> —or sick and hungry.
>
> Remember the children of the world
>> whose bellies are swollen with hunger
>> and who cannot protect themselves
>> from the systems that keep them in poverty.
>
> Remember the children
>> who are taunted and excluded
>> because of the color of their skin
>> and are helpless
>> against the racism of their society.
>
> Remember the children
>> who do not ask to be born under the shadow of bombs
>> and who have no way
>> to stop the destruction.
>
> Remember the children, O God,
>> and *make us remember what we owe to them.*
>> Through Christ our Lord. Amen.
>
> (*From* Banquet of Praise *published by Bread for the World.*)

Confirmation: Sponsors, Godparents and Parents

ROBERT D. DUGGAN

In a number of parishes and dioceses in the United States, the practice of parents presenting their children for the sacrament of confirmation has become an important issue. The questions that surround this practice come in part from the general confusion about confirmation today. They come also from problems with how roles are named and rituals are ordered in various church documents that address Christian initiation (the *Rite of Christian Initiation of Adults,* the *Rite of Infant Baptism,* the *Rite of Confirmation,* the *Code of Canon Law*). In this article we hope to resolve some of these questions and point out some basic pastoral-liturgical principles that should be respected.

TERMINOLOGY

The Roman texts that deal with initiation use the Latin term *sponsor* in regard to the person who walks with a catechumen beginning at the rite of acceptance into the order of catechumens and throughout the period of the catechumenate. *Sponsor* is also used in the rite of reception of baptized Christians into the full communion of the Catholic church. In these cases, the Latin *sponsor* is rendered in English by "sponsor." Otherwise, in the context of our initiatory sacraments, the Latin document uses the term *patrinus*.

In liturgical books the English translation of *patrinus*, however, is consistently differentiated. "Godparent" is used when the context refers to baptism and "sponsor" is used when the reference is to confirmation. In the code of canon law, on the other hand, *patrinus* is translated as "sponsor" in reference to both baptism and confirmation.

What was in the minds of the translators in making such decisions? Perhaps there was a desire to accommodate popular usage; perhaps it was felt that *patrinus* carries two separate meanings. Whatever the rationale, the result has been a blurring of a fundamental liturgical value.

TWO SACRAMENTS: ONE *PATRINUS*

The consistent use of *patrinus* in the rites of both baptism and confirmation reflects an appreciation for the intimate connection between these two sacraments of initiation. The normative expectation of both the liturgical books and the code of canon law is that the same person(s) would fulfill the role of *patrinus* (godparent/sponsor) at both baptism and confirmation. This is most clearly evident in the RCIA where both sacraments are required to be celebrated at the same time. The code reflects the same expectation when it states, "It is desirable that the one who undertook the role of sponsor *[patrinus]* at baptism be sponsor *[patrinus]* for confirmation" (canon 893.2). The *Rite of Confirmation* also states:

> In view of contemporary pastoral circumstances, it is desirable that the godparent *[patrinus]* at baptism, if present, also be the sponsor *[patrinus]* at confirmation. . . . This change expresses more clearly the relationship between baptism and confirmation and also makes the function and responsibility of the sponsor *[patrinus]* more effective. (5)

It is clear, then, that the Latin usage of *patrinus* in the context of both baptism and confirmation reflects a consistent value not only enshrined in canonical and liturgical law but also having substantial theological weight in view of the integral unity of the sacraments of initiation. From this perspective it is an anomaly—perhaps even an aberration—for anyone other than the baptismal godparent to present someone for confirmation. Our use of the English word "sponsor" in the context of confirmation may be an accommodation to current usage, but it masks the expectation of the church that the baptismal godparent will be the one to stand with his or her godchild at the second sacrament of initiation.[1]

SOUND PASTORAL PRACTICE

Church law, while it legislates an ideal, also recognizes the realities of life that sometimes make attainment of that ideal impossible. Hence, there are provisions for someone other than the baptismal godparent to present a candidate for confirmation. Years of carelessness have accustomed us to this aberrant practice so that it strikes us today as normal. Confirmation sponsors are routinely chosen without reference to one's baptismal godparent.

A better practice—one that is pastorally, liturgically and theologically more appropriate—seems called for when the baptismal godparent is not able to fulfill the expected role of *patrinus* at confirmation. The renewed *Rite of Confirmation* offers such an opportunity in its suggestion that the parents may present their child for confirmation themselves: "Even the parents themselves may present their children for confirmation. It is for the local ordinary to determine diocesan practice in the light of local circumstances" (5).

The suggestion is not that the parents are acting in the role of *patrinus,* since it is clear that parents are forbidden to take the role of godparent (canon 874.5) at baptism or "sponsor" at confirmation (893.1). What is being proposed, apparently, is that in the absence of the baptismal godparent, it is better to do without a confirmation sponsor and have the parents present their child for the sacrament.

This is the reverse of what is envisioned by the RCIA: In the initiation of children of catechetical age, the RCIA presumes that the parents will stand with their child during the initiation process. It is only in the absence of the parents that a sponsor presents the child; the sponsor does not pretend to be the parent (260, 265). So, too, in the rite of confirmation, the parents would present their child for confirmation but not pretend to play the role of godparent/sponsor. (Nowhere, by the way, is a candidate for confirmation *required* to find a new sponsor if the baptismal godparent is unavailable.)

There is room for debate over which is the better alternative to the missing baptismal godparent: the child's parent or a new sponsor. Some who lament the absence of any role for the parents in the rite of confirmation argue for using them whenever the baptismal godparent is missing. This seems especially appropriate when the child is confirmed at the time of first eucharist, as all of the reformed documents suggest ought to happen. Others point to situations, especially during adolescent confirmation, when—in the absence of the baptismal godparent—the choice of someone other than the parents to present the child may be advisable.

In weighing these alternatives, one must consider the value of replacing the baptismal godparent with a new sponsor against that of highlighting the parental role. In this latter case, the parents stand as presenters of the child; there is no sponsor other than the missing baptismal godparent.

All of these considerations serve to highlight how anomalous is the current practice of disconnecting confirmation from baptism. The farther removed in years the two sacraments become, the more complicated are our compensatory attempts to adjust to the abnormality. Taking confirmation out of its proper sequence between baptism and eucharist worsens the situation. The wisdom of the Roman tradition again emerges and reminds us that only grave reasons should lead us to abandon the ancient unity and sequence of the three sacraments of initiation.

Not without solid reasons has the reform of the Second Vatican Council insisted that baptism, confirmation and eucharist are initiatory sacraments and ought to be celebrated in that order, without unnecessary separation. Others have documented[2] the conciliar, canonical and liturgical legislation—not to mention the theological and pastoral reasons—supporting the importance of preserving the integrity of our sacraments of initiation. These reflections on who should present a candidate for delayed confirmation serve to remind us how important it is to work for full implementation of the initiatory vision of the Second Vatican Council.

Endnotes

1. We are using the singular here for the sake of convenience, although we recognize that in many cases the plural would be more appropriate in view of there being both a godmother and a godfather.

2. See especially Michael J. Bahloff, "Age for Confirmation: Canonical Evidence," Jurist 45 (1985) 549–87. Also Mark Searle, *The Church Speaks about Sacraments with Children,* (Chicago: Liturgy Training Publications, 1990).

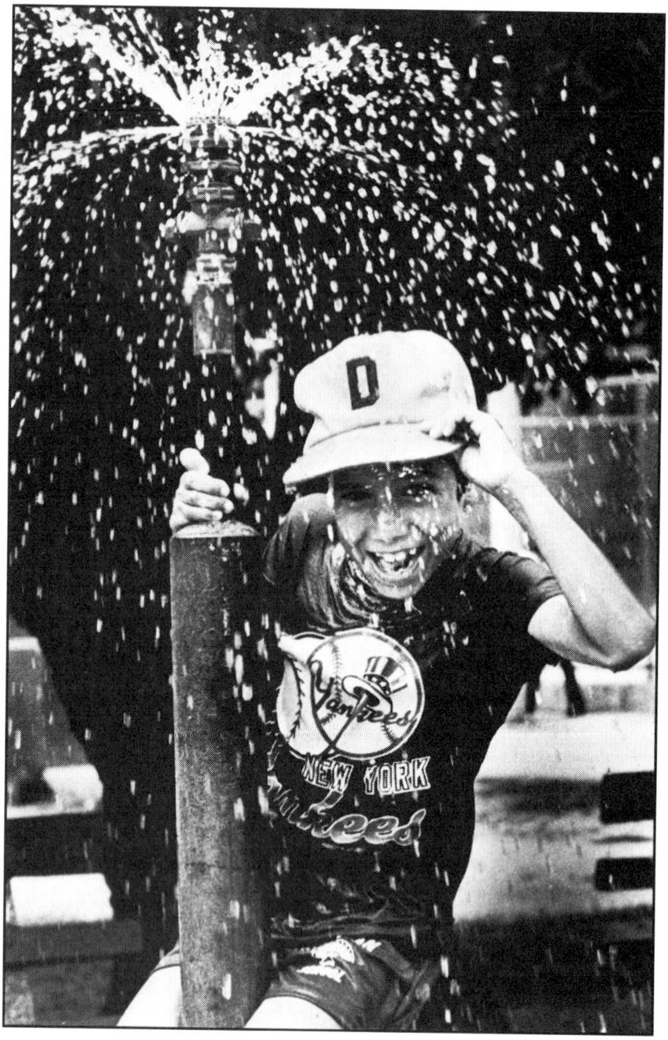
D
Yankees
NEW YORK
Yankees

PART THREE:

Pastoral Issues in Implementing the Rite

Prebaptismal and Postbaptismal Catechesis in Early Childhood

JEANETTE LUCINIO

Traditionally the church has regarded seven as the age of rationality, the age when children become capable of being taught and catechized. Yet many experts in catechetics say that growth in faith begins for the child at the moment of birth. They see the crib as the awakening place where strong perceptions about the world, about self and about God are formed. They quote the Italian adage that says, "God and the child speak the same language."[1]

READINESS AND POTENTIAL

The first six years of life are filled with tremendous bursts of development, from muscle coordination to mastery of a language. Much interest has been paid in recent years to child care, to early childhood development and to education. But we have not given the same attention to the development of the child's spiritual life. Perhaps we believe that the young child is incapable of a religious life that as adults we equate with our own rational, analytical belief.

As a teacher of young children for many years, I concur with those who describe the religious experience of preschoolers as intuitive, contemplative, affective, unified and deep.[2]

In her book, *The Religious Potential of the Child,* Sofia Cavalletti, an Italian scripture scholar and a pioneer in the field of understanding the spirituality of children, says: "The manifestations of serene and peaceful joy the children display in meeting with the world of God lead us to maintain that the religious experience responds to a deep hunger in the child."[3] This mysterious bond between God and the child seems to exist long before any religious instruction. Joy is and should be the main characteristic of the religious life of the young child. Children hunger for infinite love.

> I think the best mother and the best father have their limits, after all. With God the children have found the right partner for them.[4]

The biblical announcements of the prophets, "Be joyful! Do not fear! God is near!" are proclamations for childhood. Young children need to be told over and over that they are loved. It is in loving the child that we create the atmosphere in which the child can love God.

WHAT ADULTS TEACH, WHAT CHILDREN LEARN

The task of parents or others who accompany children is to model faith for them. Religious educator John Westerhoff says that children are brought to the faith through the modeling of others. Without modeling they may never give expression to their love.

Theological concepts are beyond the grasp of little children. To say, "Jesus is God," "Christ is God," "The Holy Spirit is God" is to say there are lots of gods. Children understand things literally, and literalism about theology breeds confusion and creates a need for much unlearning and relearning later. A highly cognitive approach to catechesis for young children needs to be drastically modified. Their willingness to believe everything compounds the danger of our feeding intellectual data to their eager ears. Just listen to a preschooler exposed to an overzealous parent or catechist. Hearsay of heaven leads to the physical resolution, "God is the man on the moon. He has a round head and bent ears. Sometimes he slips behind a cloud to have something to eat. He goes down at night to see shepherds and talk to them."[5] When asked what some of the things were that Jesus told us to do and not do, one child responded, "Don't talk with your mouth full." Children mix up family rules with basic Christian principles. It is important that we *not teach too much too soon*.

Psychological research has emphasized the importance of the preschool years for shaping the personality. Faith development occurs simultaneously with this growth. Naturally, as parents and educators we want to help in this process. Overeagerness on our part can be detrimental if we imagine that the task is to provide religious content in the form of many Bible stories, for example. Development in faith and the catechetical instruction that accompanies it is lifelong. It is a continuing process that takes place within the community, and for the young child this first community is the family.[6]

THE RELIGIOUS WORLD OF THE CHILD

The child's religious world is vastly different from that of the adult. Years can separate the adult from the peaceful, open relationship with God that is natural to the young child. Struggles and questions of faith often act as a screen to God to whom the child responds as the really real.

Cavalletti remarks that the essence of the child is the element that imposes the severest discipline on the adult.[7] Anyone seriously involved with the journey of faith of children will be driven to one's knees. A sense of the need to strip away years of accumulation of religious baggage brings one to beg for the grace to see again with new eyes "the one thing necessary"

(Luke 11:42) at the heart of the Christian mystery. This calls for study and prayer. If we allow them, children themselves will be our teachers.

Then what are we led to do? Cavalletti says that when we are dealing with children, we should speak more of proclamation and evangelization than of catechesis. This is the child's first encounter with the word of God, and its presentation deserves all the elements proper to the *kerygma,* the first announcement. The receivers of this announcement are both the child *and* the adult.

The Jewish-Christian proclamation is founded upon an event. The soil that receives the seed of the word of God is the community reflecting upon this event. Such soil can produce only if the community leans forward in the posture of listening. Listening is leaning toward others, openness and receptivity toward all around us. The capacity to listen prevents us from revolving around ourselves. Listening in community is always an enriching experience. Because children listen in a different manner than adults, listening with them allows us to encounter the word of God with newness.

INITIATORY SYMBOLS NOURISH THE CHILD

> Let your words be few but great in weight, above all with the youngest children. (Sofia Cavalletti)

There is an adult conviction that children are not capable of receiving the great realities of faith. Maybe we are not serious enough with children. Theology is not secret knowledge for the elite. If we are unable to converse about life and death and God with children (or the uneducated), perhaps we should question ourselves. As we get closer to the core of things, we will probably discover that our inability to talk about big things came from our own immaturity.

Children vary in readiness to receive the good news of faith. Because they are fond of ritual and repetition, we need not hesitate to make available the sacred signs and actions again and again. The ability to read signs is like learning a new language. It opens up for a child, as it does for an adult, the awareness of sacred reality.

In liturgy, the church has always depicted transcendent realities in images, symbols and signs. The restoration of the *Rite of Christian Initiation of Adults* has renewed this practice for the entire church. Once again we are aware of the ancient tradition of radically drawing all ages to the mystery of Christ through experience and reflection. This has always been the most effective way of instruction for children of catechetical and precatechetical age. It is the beginning of a lifelong journey that opens the way to veneration of the mystery yet never claims to define it fully. To use signs is to give great reverence and space to the individual's personal work of absorption. The method of sign educates the parent or catechist in humility.[8]

What are the symbols? I suggest that the best experiential signs and symbols for small children are the time-honored symbols of sacramental initiation: water, light, fragrant oil, touch, food, presence and belonging. Children need to experience them and reflect on them. Merely speaking about them will not touch children in a lasting way. Signs of initiation are signs of life surrounding the child in her or his experience. All of our sacramental signs rise out of ordinary life and do not add to or subtract from the sacredness already there. We need not create an artificial link between daily events and prayer. Early in life a child begins to read gestures, facial expressions and parental attitudes as a language without words. This is the initial vocabulary they master, understanding it first dimly, then clearly getting the message. Caring adults clasp the infant's hand and extend their arms to the child. The infant responds by opening arms wide in a gesture that says, "Pick me up and bring me close to you, into warm, comfortable contact with your body. I belong to you, and you belong to me." Gestures of touch and of welcome confirm within the child those first images of God, conveying the message, "I love you, and you are mine."

Because sharing food conveys a sense of caring, mealtime is another powerful symbolic moment. The little child who sits in the high chair at the table participates in more than food. If the meal begins with prayer, the child joins in by being part of it.

Bedtime is another strong moment of awareness for a child. The beautiful habit of blessing the forehead of the child with the sign of the cross leaves a powerful imprint for the rest of her or his life. The parent or caring adult is affected as well by this carryover from the signification of the baptismal rite. The sign of the cross on the forehead is deeply imbedded in the memory of the child. It is one of my earliest memories and prepared me for a sacramental sense of life.

Catechesis of the Symbols. Playing in the sunlight, awaiting the arrival of visitors, singing around a birthday cake with candles, lighting a candle in a darkened room, making things together—these are experiences that delight children. Christmas is a wonderful time to reflect with them on the beauty and joy of light.

When introducing the baptismal signs, Cavalletti suggests that children easily grasp the natural link between the Easter liturgy of light around the paschal candle and the Christmas celebration of Jesus' birth as the light of the world, if their attention is called to it. A large candle is lit, and the children enjoy the light, the far-reaching light. The children are called one by one to come and light their own candles from the great Christ candle. At home, the baptismal candle or the Christ candle burning brightly may serve as a reminder of the light of the world on anniversaries, at important meals, with guests, during high seasons or in troubled times.

A parent, guardian or catechist may say: "The light comes to us also through the book of God's word. This book contains the good news of God's love for us. The word of God's love gives light to our hearts. Jesus said, 'Everything I have heard from my Father, I have told you'" (John 15:15).

The work of children is play. It occupies a great part of their life. Children play their way into awareness. Burning candles at table, sharing a cup with real wine on special occasions, blessing one another for departures, arrivals, sleeping and waking, using oil around the home for the usual things, baking or eating bread and happily washing oneself or slaking one's thirst with water—all these things pondered, appreciated and discussed give religious nourishment to young children. The awakening of a religious sense takes place at the heart of life. It is not something built *on* natural experience but is developed *within* it, uncovering the depth, origin and purpose of the natural. If we allow them, children can lead us to the face of God.

Endnotes

1. Carol Dittberner, "The Pure Wonder of Young Lives," *Sojourners* (January 1987), 21.

2. Barbara Schmich, "The Formation of Children," *Assembly* 13 (June 1987).

3. Sofia Cavalletti, *The Religious Potential of the Child* (Chicago: Liturgy Training Publications, 1992), 45.

4. Carol Dittberner and Cathy Maresca, "Teaching Us the Source of Joy: An Interview with Sofia Cavalletti," *Sojourners* (January 19871, 23.

5. Ronald Goldman, *Readiness for Religion* (New York: Seabury Press, 1970), 80.

6. Christiane Brusselmans, with Edward Wakin, *A Parents' Guide: Religion for Little Children* (Huntington, Indiana: Our Sunday Visitor, Inc., 1977), 150–51.

7. Cavalletti, *Religious Potential,* 47

8. Ibid., 158–67

Caring for the Anawim: Catechetical Age Children

DON NEUMANN

This story is true. In other stories, the roles may be reversed and the circumstances may be different, but the patterns will be quite familiar.

There was no particular reason they didn't get their firstborn baptized. There was a multitude of reasons. They were married three years when the news came. Jobs were going well. They were talking about the possibility of having children—they thought they could handle the responsibilities of being parents. That was when it happened. A baby was on the way. Not really a surprise, but not exactly when they had hoped for. They were happy and nervous at the same time.

The pregnancy went well. The baby was born. But like so many young Catholic couples, they did not attend church regularly in those early years of marriage. So many things seemed to take precedence. With the birth of the baby, thoughts of church began to arise again (especially through the interventions of a loving, prodding grandmother). "When are you going to have the baby baptized?" And without much forethought they answered, "Oh, we haven't talked about it yet. I guess we'll have to call the church and find out when we can do it."

But they never called. The father of the child was never hot on religion anyway, and the Catholic mother put her faith on the back burner while she tended to the care that she needed to give her new family to build strong foundations. They were good people—genuinely good. Religion was just not a big part of their lives.

After a few more years, another baby was on the way. Loving grandparents and aunts and uncles repeatedly asked about baptism—fortunately not in a guilt-provoking way. Guilt ensued nonetheless. She asked him early in the second pregnancy about the possibility of baptism for the children, and he lovingly agreed. She breathed a sigh of relief, thinking that now would be a good time to get her faith in order too. Only one thing stood in the way—the expectation of the church that she have a living faith and that she would pledge to share that faith with the children as long as they were under her parental influence.

When she called the parish, she got the usual story: "First you have to register and participate in parish life. Then there are classes for baptismal preparation, and during that preparation we will tell you the dates of baptism." She made an appointment to see the priest, and after the interview, for no particular reason other than the general burden of it all, she decided not to attend the baptism class. She dropped out but still attended Mass periodically with two small children until the first child was six and the second child was four.

By now she had more time and genuinely desired to get involved with her church in a fuller way. The children were getting older and beginning to ask uncomfortable questions like "Why don't you go up to receive the host when everyone else does, Mommy?" and "Will we be able to go up and receive someday?" She went to talk with the priest again. This time he spoke to her about a process for preparing children of teachable age for baptism called the catechumenate for children. The words sounded strange, but she was intrigued, and the priest was excited about it, so she thought it might be worth a try.

She went to the first session for parents and children who were to be part of the children's catechumenate. She was surprised to see that she was not the only one in this situation. The room was filled with 16 other families who had not had their children baptized as infants, and for a split second she had a feeling that maybe she *did* belong to the Catholic family after all. For the first time she felt part of a family of Catholics who wanted to take their faith seriously, even if it was a day later than some others.

She enjoyed the first session. The children liked it too. A new beginning, indeed.

She continued to attend Mass but now much more regularly. They all took part in the catechumenate for children. The children belonged to a group of young boys and girls who knew that they were preparing to become part of the brothers and sisters of Jesus in baptism. The experience marked a welcome shift for their family from being *apart from* the church to being *a part of* the church.

Curiously, it was on the Sunday of the rite of acceptance of children into the order of catechumens that the mother realized that she never really chose to leave the church; she just began drifting. She let other things attract her attention. During those years her loved ones took all her time and attention. Going to church and getting the children baptized just didn't seem important. Unintentionally she began to see herself as a bad Catholic and an irresponsible Catholic parent because she failed to follow the customary patterns of getting the children baptized as babies and raising them in the church afterward. Only on this Sunday, at this moment, did it strike her that for years she had perceived herself as a fallen away Catholic and an embarrassment to her family. And then, suddenly, out of the blue during the rite of acceptance it struck her: "I am not a bad Catholic parent for waiting to get my child baptized. I am trying to do my best *now* with all the faith I can muster, and I am not an embarrassment to the faith. I am just part of a different set of circumstances."

During the rite of acceptance, the guilt and shame she had felt during all those years of not measuring up were brushed away like a gentle breeze, as the parish church celebrated a rite of *welcome* for children.

CAUTION: RELIGIOUS "FULL-TIMERS"

For those of us who are actively involved in the pastoral implementation of the catechumenate for children of catechetical age, several significant issues surfaced in the story of this family.

First, a catechumenate for children is an opportunity for the parish to grow in faith. It is not simply more work for the staff. There are many reasons why people don't have children baptized as infants. The issue is not "Why didn't you do this at infancy?" Rather, it is joy that these parents want to take the responsibility now for sharing their faith with their children, and that their children want to share it. The times that people come to God are not predictable. The role of the church is to be there with open arms whenever people decide to come.

Second, the catechumenate for children is to facilitate the journey of children and their families into a closer relationship with God in Jesus and into the family of the church. It's a family affair. The opportunity to affect the life of a whole family is a precious moment for both the family and the local church. Cherish it!

Third, if Jesus left to us the ministry of reconciliation, then we may begin to see that the catechumenate for children is one of those opportunities to focus on reconciliation in truly relational terms. No one who prepared the rites of initiation for adults or children of catechetical age ever dreamed that the circumstance mentioned in this article could occur. But it did. It always surprises us! The catechumenate for children may be yet another way for the community of faith to celebrate the reconciliation of all persons and all creation into the mystery of Christ. If so, we had better be prepared to be the reconciling community of the Lord. Reconciliation is first of all relational—between real persons in real situations. To miss the opportunity of healing families with broken faith is a great tragedy. So don't miss it! Perhaps families with children of catechetical age are prime candidates for the healing that only Jesus and the first sacrament of reconciliation (baptism) can offer. Making people whole is the business of the ministry of reconciliation, and anything that makes that happen is worthwhile.

Fourth, the restoration of the three sacraments of initiation in their proper order makes the statement that the church is willing to have a varied praxis of initiation. Infants who are baptized receive the initiation sacraments in one order and pattern. Children of catechetical age celebrate the initiation sacraments as a whole. Nowhere in the rite is the permission given to postpone confirmation so that "they can make it with their peers." It is not only faulty pastoral practice to disregard the ritual rubrics, but it makes a misleading theological statement as well. The rite prefers that children of catechetical age be treated "like adults" in the celebration of the sacraments of initiation. That is why the chapter "Christian Initiation of Children Who Have Reached Catechetical Age" is found in the *Rite of Christian Initiation of Adults.*

Fifth, just as the National Statutes (#24) now call for a monthly meeting of the newly initiated until the anniversary of their baptism, so parishes will have to consider how they will support and nurture the newly baptized children of catechetical age and their families until the anniversary of their baptism and beyond. By the adoption of statutes such as these, the church is saying clearly, "Becoming a Christian is wonderful, but remaining a faithful Christian is imperative." It is never as easy to remain a Catholic as it is to become one. Like any commitment, it takes us regularly to the cross and empty tomb.

CONCLUSION

What should be the content of catechesis for the children's catechumenate? What are the best methods for relaying the faith of the church? What is the role of imagination? The issues surrounding religious experience and religious language are just a few important things that still need attention before a children's catechumenate can be successful. But the reflections of the story that began this article still give us pause. Why did the parents delay the baptism and still feel guilty about it?

After we have learned the rites and the process that make the children's catechumenate work, it will be the exceptions to the rule that prove our true understanding. It is in the care we show for these exceptions that our faithfulness to the mission of Jesus will stand out.

What Should We Ask of Child Catechumens?

RITA BURNS SENSEMAN

In his book *On Becoming a Catholic: The Challenge of Christian Initiation,* Regis Duffy poses the question, "What should we ask of catechumens?"[1] In other words, what should the Christian community ask or expect of its catechumens to ensure that they will honestly and fruitfully receive the sacraments of initiation? In this article I ask a modified version of this question: "What should we ask of child catechumens?" This question arises from a current situation: Children of catechetical age, either with or without their parents, are approaching the parish and requesting initiation. The purpose of this article is to assert that the Christian community must ask conversion of its child catechumens. "The Christian initiation of these children requires a conversion that is personal and somewhat developed, in proportion to their age" (*Rite of Christian Initiation of Adults,* 253). Conversion is the heart of the catechumenate, and the church believes that even young catechumens can enter into catechumenal formation. After making general comments, I will direct my attention to children of junior high school age, the group with which I have had the most experience.

THREE SUPPOSITIONS

The first step in responding to the question, "What should we ask of child catechumens?" is to establish three suppositions. The first is that the child catechumens "are capable of receiving and nurturing a personal faith and of recognizing an obligation in conscience" (RCIA, 252). That is, the children have "attained the use of reason" and they also have a desire for receiving and nurturing faith.

Second, the church holds that because these children have reached the age of reason (seven years), they are able to "profess faith and undergo the catechumenal formation" (*Code of Canon Law*, canon 852.1). Though they are not adults in their level of personal maturity, because "children who have reached the use of reason are considered, for the purpose of Christian initiation, to be adults (canon 852.1), their formation should follow the general pattern of the ordinary catechumenate" (RCIA, National Statutes, 18). This means that our expectations of child catechumens should be comparable to those we have for adult catechumens; at the same time, expectations should be developmentally appropriate for each child. Statute 18 also means that all that is said in the RCIA applies to children as well as to adults.

The third presupposition is that this article will not attempt to describe fully the theories of child development and conversion when discussing the conversion process of the child catechumens. I will offer indications that suggest when a child has experienced and is in the process of conversion.

TWO HISTORICAL PRECEDENTS

The church has, throughout its history, asked young catechumens to undergo catechumenal formation and conversion. In the early church, Tertullian referred to children being baptized. He claimed that children should come for baptism "when they are growing up, when they are learning, when they are being taught what they are coming to: Let them be made

Christians when they have become competent to know Christ."[2] Tertullian's statement suggests two elements in the children's catechumenal formation. First, children have the competency and ability to know Christ. Second, children are not to be made Christians until they understand what it means to know Christ. "To know Christ" implies much more than an intellectual understanding of Christology. Rather, "to know Christ" means that one understands Jesus' message, including the call to conversion and discipleship. According to Tertullian, children are among those called to conversion and discipleship.[3]

In the *Apostolic Tradition,* Hippolytus also speaks of conversion of heart and of lifestyle. When he refers to the initiation of children, he says that if "the children can speak for themselves, they shall do so."[4] This indicates that the children can speak about a conversion of heart and lifestyle comparable to that of the adults who are questioned and who answer in a similar way.

CONVERSION AND THE CHILD CATECHUMEN

Though the church asks conversion of young catechumens in the same way it asks conversion of adult catechumens, the church also recognizes that these children "cannot yet be treated as adults because, at this stage of their lives, they are dependent on their parents or guardians" (RCIA, 253). Nevertheless, we expect the child catechumens to experience conversion so that they may be able to celebrate honestly and fruitfully the sacraments of initiation.

In catechumenal formation, conversion means a change of heart, a change in lifestyle and attitudes, a turning toward Jesus Christ. Yet, what sort of change or turning do we expect in child catechumens? The same we expect of an adult? Ultimately, we do expect the same sort of change in that we expect conversion. However, conversion for a child will be different than for an adult. A child has a different kind of life experience than an adult, but enough experience to enter into the conversion process. The stories that children bring to the catechumenal process reveal the depth and richness of their life experience.

Rene, Chris and Daniel brought to St. Andrew Parish beautiful and sometimes painful stories of life in a single-parent, inner-city home with six children and four grandchildren.[5] They had no trouble seeing the connection between their own life experience and the presence of Jesus. For example, during one of the pastoral interviews, the children spoke of the great many people in their home, and of the problems with their older brothers and sister that often disrupted the household. They felt that it was Jesus who helped the family in times of trouble. Daniel even related that Jesus probably helped his own mother when she was tired or upset, just as the children in Daniel's family did.

FOUR DIMENSIONS OF CONVERSION

The conversion process fostered in the catechumenate, whether it be for a child or an adult, should affect all dimensions of a person's life: affective, social, intellectual and moral.[6] The young catechumen is quite capable of conversion in each of these dimensions of life. However, recognizing that the child is still "dependent on their parents or guardians," the parent or guardian must be included in the child's conversion process whenever possible. That is not to say that conversion is dependent on the parent or guardian. At times, a parent or guardian is unwilling or unable to walk with the child through the process. Returning to the example of Rene, Chris and Daniel: Their mother was not able to participate in the formal process because of her demanding and complicated life situation. In this instance, the parish sponsor walked with the children.[7] Mrs. Jackson, who had children of ages similar to Rene, Chris and Daniel, served as a sponsor for the family. She developed a deep friendship not only with the children but also with their mother. Mrs. Jackson often helped with transportation to church and visited the family at home.

The Affective Dimension of Conversion   The affective dimension of the child's conversion is essential to the catechumenal process. The affective dimension is essential because the paschal mystery—participation in the life, death and resurrection of Jesus—is profoundly, though not exclusively, experienced at the emotional level. Since the whole of initiation is paschal in character, the catechumens must have a penetrating experience of the paschal mystery.[8] The community invites the child catechumens to enter into the mystery of Christ, not at the cognitive level but rather at the affective level. We do this by helping them to appreciate the deaths and resurrections already happening in their young lives.[9] Child catechumens need to be helped to recognize and name the experience. Child catechumens know of the power of love overcoming death through the love and example of parents, family, and friends. Rene, age 15, knew that her mother was often angry, sad and tired, but she also saw that her mother somehow was able to keep their family together. Rene, as well as her brother and sister, came to see in their mother's strength the power and promise of the paschal mystery.

Affective conversion is a movement from the knowledge of God to the experience of God. We do not try to teach children the doctrine of the Trinity in cognitive terms; rather, we teach God by helping them to experience and recognize where God is bringing life from death.[10] This means that we share with the catechumens our stories of God creating, loving, making promises, caring and forgiving. We share with them stories of Jesus healing people, freeing people, teaching people and feeding people, and of his suffering, dying and rising. We share with them stories of the Holy Spirit working in the past and still today, giving people life, strength, courage and power.

This sharing is done through celebrations of the word at the Sunday liturgy and at other times of catechumenal formation. As we proclaim the word, we invite the catechumens to enter into the living word and to relate it to their own life story. Once the catechumens have experienced and identified the action of God in their own lives, as Rene, Chris and Daniel did, they have begun to know the paschal mystery. The child has moved from cognitive knowledge of God to an affective experience of God: The child has undergone affective conversion.

The Social Dimension of Conversion   For the child, the social dimension of conversion means moving from seeing herself or himself as an individual connected only to parents and family to perceiving herself or himself as a person who is also a part of a larger Christian community. At this level of conversion, the child comes to understand that, as a sister or brother of Jesus, she or he is united with others through the power of the Spirit. The child comes to a sense of oneness with others both in the local Christian community and in the world.

The social dimension of conversion was exemplified by Anthony, age 13, who was very introverted and withdrawn when he first came to St. Andrew Parish. Anthony and his father came to the catechumenal sessions together, and for the first few weeks, Anthony spoke to and interacted with others very little. By the following year, Anthony became a leader in the youth group, and he was always one of the first to share in discussion in the catechumenal group. He eagerly volunteered to work at the youth-group dances and to help cook the Thanksgiving meal at our parish's residence for senior citizens. He had obviously come to feel a oneness with others in his community.

The Intellectual Dimension of Conversion   The third dimension of the child's conversion is intellectual conversion. Referring to the catechumenate, the RCIA directs that

> a suitable catechesis is [to be] provided by priests and deacons or by catechists and others of the faithful, planned to be gradual and complete in its coverage, accommodated to the liturgical year and solidly supported by celebrations of the word. This catechesis leads the catechumens not only to an appropriate acquaintance with dogmas and precepts but also to a profound sense of the mystery of salvation in which they desire to participate. (#75.1)

Mark Searle points out that a key word in this statement is "suitable."[11] The intellectual dimension of conversion should be suitable for a child's age and maturity. "Suitable" means that the quality of what is taught is more important than the quantity.[12] Children should not be expected to comprehend every dogma and precept of the church. Instead, catechesis centered around the word, the primary Christian symbols and the creed will assist them in understanding the mystery of Christ alive in their midst.

In addition, the liturgical rites for the children are an integral element of the catechesis that leads to "a profound sense of the mystery of salvation" (RCIA, 75.1). The symbols found in the various rites speak quite powerfully to a child. For example, in the rite of acceptance into the order of catechumens, the children are signed with the sign of the cross on the forehead and then on all their other senses (RCIA, 266–268). Most children have no difficulty understanding the profundity of the symbol. After having experienced this rite, the young catechumens at St. Perpetua Parish were invited to express how they felt about the rite. The children were able to articulate the meaning of the symbol. Sandra, age 13, said, "It felt like Jesus was covering me. He is on my head, and hands, and eyes, and ears. It's like he is surrounding me. I feel like he'll always be there for me."[13] Thoughts expressed in this way are an indication that the child has a "sense of the mystery of salvation." This points to the intellectual conversion of the child.

The Moral Dimension of Conversion The fourth dimension of the child's conversion, the moral dimension, is about personal response. As the child begins to experience the paschal mystery and feel a part of the Christian community, she or he will feel prompted to respond in faith. The church looks for the catechumens "to bear witness to the faith . . . to practice love of neighbor, even at the cost of self-renunciation" (RCIA, 75.2). To "bear witness to the faith" means to participate actively in the paschal mystery, which the child professes to believe. For the child, this means to give unselfishly of herself or himself to others. Child catechumens can do this by being more helpful at home and school; by doing kind deeds for parents, siblings, grandparents and others; and by participating in the life of the church. These types of activities might indicate moral conversion.

Moral conversion was evidenced in a definite way by Matt, age 14. After entering into the catechumenal process, Matt and his mother could be found at almost every Christian service activity at St. Perpetua Parish: They worked at the fish fry, which was a fund-raiser to help feed hungry people in the local community; they worked at the temporary shelter for the homeless the week it was at our parish; they served at the Right-to-Life baby shower. Also, Matt's mother described how friendly Matt had become with their neighbors. Matt's response in action and attitude indicated he had experienced moral conversion.

SUMMARY

What should we ask of child catechumens? Conversion. But what we ask of our child catechumens should be no less than what we ask of ourselves. The Christian community should ask for ongoing conversion of the faithful. If we want our child catechumens to celebrate the sacraments of initiation honestly and fruitfully, then the faithful must do the same. The challenge is not to separate our expectations of the child catechumens from the expectations we have of the faithful. This will lead both the catechumens and the baptized to honest, fruitful, lifegiving celebration of the sacraments and to a lived response of service.[14]

Endnotes

1. Regis Duffy, *On Becoming a Catholic. The Challenge of Christian Initiation* (San Francisco: Harper and Row, 1984), xi.

2. Ernest Evans, ed., trans., *Tertullian's Homily on Baptism* (Cambridge: University Printing House 1964), 39.

3. Ibid.

4. Burton Scott Easton, ed., trans., *The Apostolic Tradition of Hippolytus* (U.S.A.: Cambridge University Press, 1962), 45.

5. Rene, age 15; Chris, age 12; and Daniel, age 11, were part of the catechumenal group at St. Andrew Parish in Indianapolis, Indiana. St. Andrew is an inner-city parish of approximately 400 families.

6. Duffy, vii.

7. When a parent, guardian or family member is not available to walk through the catechumenal process with the child catechumen, then a parish sponsor may be the one to walk with the child. Regardless of whether or not there is a family member present, however, there should always be a parish sponsor. An ideal situation occurs when a parish family sponsors a catechumenal family.

8. Duffy, 85–86.

9. Carol Dittberner, "The Pure Wonder of Young Lives," *Sojourners* (January 1987), 20, 24–25.

10. Duffy, 99

11. Mark Searle, "Conversion and Initiation into Faith Growth," *Christian Initiation Resources Reader,* Moya Gullage and James T. Morgan, eds. (New York: William H. Sadlier, Inc., 1984), vol. 1, 71. Though Searle is referring to the 1974 edition of the RCIA, the word "suitable" appears in the 1988 edition also.

12. Ibid.

13. Sandra was involved in the catechumenal process at St. Perpetua Parish in Waterford, Michigan. St. Perpetua is a

suburban parish of 900 families. Sandra expressed the thoughts quoted in this article during the "breaking open the word" session after the rite of acceptance into the order of catechumens.

14. Sacramental Theology class lecture by Regis Duffy, University of Notre Dame, 24 June 1988.

How Did We Get Where We Are, and Where Do We Go from Here?

FRANK C. SOKOL

The catechetical renewal of this century, with its emphasis on cultural adaptation, maturing in faith, the engagement of the whole person and the primacy of the word, shows that the ecclesial ministry of catechizing children is refined by each successive generation of Christians. Just as the reign of God is discovered anew by successive generations, so is catechesis renewed. Our focus is catechesis in our time in history and how that catechesis relates to the catechumenate for children.

CONTEMPORARY CATECHESIS

Of the many things that could be said about the various twentieth-century catechetical movements, I make five observations that represent a limited but significant picture:

1. Catechesis Respects Human Experience. It encourages critical reflection upon it. A major breakthrough at the beginning of this century enabled a refinement of the severe dichotomy between the human and divine, the immanent and transcendent. This began with the philosophical contribution that Maurice Blondel offered in his doctoral dissertation of 1893, *L'Action*. For Blondel, *action* was the driving force, the dynamism in all of life, the basis for reflection upon life itself. The transcendent is not only extrinsic to the human person but is also intrinsic to being human. In this way, the divine can be understood as the deepest dimension of being human.

As applied to catechesis, human experience becomes the grist for the formation and development of faith. Our contemporary catechetical methods begin with an exploration into experience in order to draw from it what is most authentically human, thereby discovering the divine as well.

2. Catechesis Links Human and Religious Experience.

Recently I observed my sister sitting with her son, 3-year-old Adam. Together they were examining the contents of a bag that Adam had filled during a walk through the backyard. Rocks, leaves, an old tennis ball, a piece of clothesline, some bark from the apple tree—each item was looked at, felt and discussed. Near the end of this grace-filled time, a simple statement was offered to Adam: "God made the whole world and wants us to take care of it." A connection was made. Adam entered his role as co-creator with God.

A classic connection story in the Scriptures occurs in the journey taken by the two disciples on the road to Emmaus. From the confusion, doubt and pain of their human experience, Jesus Christ drew out a meaning: "Didn't the messiah have to undergo all this in order to enter the reign?" A connection was made.

Catechesis takes the scattered points of human existence and connects them so that a design emerges for sacred and meaningful living.

3. Catechesis Prepares for Ongoing Conversion.

Conversion is the heart of the gospel message and of the Christian life. By instigating reflection on our experience and by making connections among those experiences, catechesis acts as an occasion for conversion. It uncovers the longings, dissatisfactions, incompleteness, brokenness, passion and needs of human life that are some of the initiators of conversion.

4. Catechesis Is Based on the Bible and Liturgy. The church has moved in this century from pietism to a greater focus on liturgy and sacred scripture. Advances in ritual studies and the theology of story have demonstrated the formative and constitutive functions of liturgy and scripture. These advances opened the more symbol-making and less discursive attributes of human activity as essential factors in the formation of faith.

5. Catechesis Is Family Oriented. In Peter L. Berger's and Thomas Luckmann's *The Social Construction of Reality: A Treatise in the Sociology of Knowledge,* a distinction is made between primary and secondary socialization. The authors assert that no secondary socialization can have the same formative influence as a primary socialization. Applied to catechesis as maturing in the faith, our traditional catechetical structures are secondary socializations. They can build only on what has already been experienced as a primary socialization in the values and beliefs of one's family.

CATECHESIS IN THE CATECHUMENATE FOR CHILDREN

When we combine our observations about contemporary catechesis in general with the vision of the order of Christian initiation, the following synthesis results: Catechesis in the catechumenate for children is based on ritual and reflection on the primary symbols of the faith and the scriptures. Such catechesis necessarily involves the ongoing conversion of the adult community, including the family.

1. Catechesis for Children Is Based on the Rite. The texts of the initiatory rites offer a vision of entering the Christian community through an ordered sequence. They also offer the structure for enacting those rites. The text itself is essentially a liturgical one.

The assumption is that the primary formative experience for the Christian and for the Christian community is the liturgy. This primary experience of Christian formation is then supported by other dimensions of the faith, such as reflection and articulation, community building, service and outreach.

This part of the vision may call for a change in the way we think about liturgy and catechesis. We have assumed that children will be formed primarily through teaching, that learning experiences are supplemented by experiences of prayer and public worship and that these liturgical layers are simply additions or "extras" to a child's formation.

Without weakening any catechetical efforts it must be acknowledged that the best of the church's tradition has made liturgy—not catechesis—the source and summit of its life. Rather than threaten the essential ministry of catechesis, we can strengthen it by realizing that the most important activity of the Christian community is to gather in faith, to reflect upon its life, to give thanks and to go back into the world for service. Catechesis leads to and flows from the central act of the community: the liturgy.

In well-planned and carefully executed rites, we learn quite naturally how to live as Christians. In the catechumenate for children the catechetical sessions flow organically from the liturgical experiences. Rather than layering liturgy upon catechesis, the believing church comes from the praying church: From their experiences of public worship, children find out how the adult community lives its faith.

2. Catechumenal Catechesis Is Based on Symbols of Faith and Scripture.
The *Rite of Christian Initiation of Adults,* 75.1, provides the direction here:

> A suitable catechesis . . . accommodated to the liturgical year and solidly supported by celebrations of the word . . . leads the catechumens not only to an appropriate acquaintance with dogmas and precepts but also to a profound sense of the mystery of salvation.

Since the mystery of salvation is lived and celebrated in the course of one complete liturgical year, it is expected that the catechumenate would be at least as long. This gives catechumens the opportunity to get the complete picture, to get a genuine sense of why and how the Christian community believes what it believes. The liturgical cycle unfolds the truths of the faith in a systematic way, drawing the community into the mystery of salvation.

The symbol of the faith—*symbolum fidei*—is an important source for catechesis. It is the identifying mark of the Christian community, the characteristics by which the believers in Jesus are known. As inquirers, children begin to develop a religious sense and a way of living their faith within Christian community. As catechumens, they move more intimately into the tradition that identifies them as Roman Catholic. Adults at this point can deal more readily with the abstractions of the creeds and dogmas. Children need to have what the creeds and dogmas express made more concrete: Trinity, for example, is learned through the sign of the cross; redemption is explained through the crucifix in their Sunday gathering place; the indwelling of the Holy Spirit is expressed through the catechumenal anointing of their bodies with oil. These are dimensions of the faith that they will be learning in their regular catechetical sessions.

3. Catechumenal Catechesis for Children Involves the Ongoing Conversion of the Adult Community. We need formation at all stages of life, not just in childhood. If we pay more attention to the ongoing conversion of adults, a result of that care will be better-formed children. Catechesis in a catechumenate for children needs to accomplish one thing: to lead them into the mystery of faith. That is done best by affording children opportunities to see, touch, feel, know and walk in that mystery as it is lived by a community of faith and as it is remembered and proclaimed through its sacred writings.

CONCLUSION

Where does all this lead us? Where do we go from here? If catechesis respects human experience and connects that experience with a process of conversion that is biblically based, liturgically founded and family oriented, then many good things are already happening. The challenge is to build on the good structures and processes. Use them. If the structures and processes cannot support the church's vision of the catechumenate, then they cannot be expected to form new Christians. The challenge is not only to design a process for the catechumenate but also to allow the catechumenal process to challenge the catechetical structure. This is where we go from here. The entire enterprise of preparing children of catechetical age for baptism has the potential for reshaping all of our catechetical endeavors. Dealing with baptism takes us, to use Aidan Kavanagh's language, to the "storm center of the universe." At this moment in our history there is a sense of calm — not a calm as in complacency, but a calm as in "before a storm." And this calm affords us a little time and space to re-form initiation policies for children, for the storm cannot be far behind. And that storm will surely sweep us into a new creation.

Conversion in Jesus Christ has to do not only with the water bath of our sons and daughters, sisters and brothers, nieces and nephews, neighbors and friends. It has to do with the very transformation of the world into the reign of God. Participating in this transformation is the unique privilege of all God's children.

Statement on the Pastoral Challenge of Implementing the *Rite of Christian Initiation of Adults* for Children Who Have Reached Catechetical Age

Recognizing the pastoral issues faced by those working with children of catechetical age, the National Conference of Catholic Bishops' (NCCB) Committees on the Liturgy and on Pastoral Research and Practices, and the United States Catholic Conference's (USCC) Committee on Education collaborated on a study of the current documents regarding Christian initiation. Their joint statement was approved on March 20, 1990, by the Administrative Committee of the National Conference of Catholic Bishops.

With the implementation of the final translation of the *Rite of Christian Initiation of Adults* (RCIA) on September 1, 1988, and the increased understanding that has been gained of this rite during the past few years, there has arisen the pastoral challenge of implementing that portion of the RCIA (part II, chapter 1) that applies to the "particular circumstances" of children who have reached catechetical age and who have not yet been initiated.

There now are many families whose adult members are being initiated, or are returning to the practice of the faith, and who have children of varying ages who have not received one or more of the sacraments of initiation. There are often, in the same family, older baptized but uncatechized children and younger children who have been neither baptized nor catechized. According to the requirements of the RCIA, these family members are to be initiated in diverse ways. Unbaptized adults will be enrolled in the catechumenate and ultimately will receive all the sacraments of initiation at the same time. Baptized but uncatechized adults will be given the necessary catechetical formation and, if circumstances warrant, may be enrolled in an adapted form of the catechumenate for the already baptized; at the appropriate time, they will receive the eucharist and/or confirmation. Baptized but uncatechized children will receive the necessary catechesis for confirmation and the eucharist and will receive these sacraments, insofar as possible, at the same time as their classmates. Unbaptized children of catechetical age will participate in a suitably adapted form of the catechumenate and, after the necessary period of formation, will receive all three sacraments of initiation at the same time. Unbaptized infants and small children will be baptized and then will participate in the usual catechetical and sacramental formation programs for those baptized in infancy.

Thus, within the same family individuals may be initiated at different times and in different ways, depending on their age, whether or not they have been baptized and the extent to which they have previously been formed in the Christian life. Those responsible for catechesis must clearly explain to families the various approaches to the Christian formation and sacramental initiation of their family members that correspond to these different factors.

The NCCB/USCC Committees on Pastoral Research and Practice, Liturgy and Education recognize the challenge that these varying situations present for pastors and religious educators. Nevertheless, the initiation of unbaptized children who have reached the age of discretion always must conform to the requirements of the *Rite of Christian Initiation of Adults*. These persons are to be admitted into a form of the catechumenate that has been adapted to the particular needs of children (see RCIA, 252–259). They will receive the three sacraments of initiation once they have been suitably formed in the Christian way of life and have established that they are ready for the sacraments (see RCIA, 256). The confirmation of such children should not be separated from the other sacraments of initiation to which it is integrally related.

Because the NCCB members have not set a uniform age for confirmation of those who were baptized as infants, it will be necessary for pastors and religious educators to explain that varying practices regarding the age of those to be confirmed and the sequence of the reception of confirmation and eucharist exist in our country. They should provide the appropriate catechesis and rites of initiation necessary for the initiation of individuals into the sacramental life of the church in conformity to diocesan regulations.

The Committees on Pastoral Research and Practices, Liturgy and Education also recognize the need for new instructional materials, methods and models to compensate for the lack of published sacramental preparation materials for older children preparing for confirmation and for lectionary-based catechesis. The Department of Education's task force preparing guidelines for catechetical materials will keep this in mind and share these needs with the publishers of catechetical materials.

The Committees on Pastoral Research and Practices, Liturgy and Education express their appreciation for all that religious educators are striving to do in the face of these pastoral challenges, and encourage them to continue informing the NCCB/USCC Committees of their pastoral experiences so that the church may provide for the faith formation of our people.

Authors

CHRISTIANE BRUSSELMANS was a leader in the implementation of the initiation process for both children and adults. She was instrumental in the founding of the North American Forum on the Catechumenate and was cofounder, with James Moudry, of the Institute for the Christian Initiation of Children. Her program of sacramental preparation for children and families, *We Celebrate the Eucharist,* is published by Silver Burdett and Ginn. Christiane Brusselmans died in 1991.

RITA BURNS SENSEMAN writes and speaks on the Christian initiation of children. She served for several years as associate director in the office of catechetics/religious education of the archdiocese of Detroit. She also was director of religious education and the catechumenate at St. Andrew Parish in Indianapolis, and St. Perpetua Parish in Waterford, Michigan.

CATHERINE DOOLEY, OP teaches in the School of Religious Studies at The Catholic University of America in Washington, D.C. She is a frequent speaker and author in the area of catechesis and the initiation of children. Her recent book, *To Listen and Tell* (Washington D.C.: Pastoral Press, 1993) is a commentary on the introduction to the *Lectionary for Masses with Children.*

ROBERT D. DUGGAN is pastor of St. Rose of Lima Parish, Gaithersburg, Maryland. A frequent speaker and writer on Christian initiation, he edited *Conversion and the Catechumenate* (New York: Paulist Press, 1984), coauthored the *Catholic Faith Inventory* (Paulist Press, 1986) with Kenneth Boyack and Paul Huesing, and coauthored *Christian Initiation of Children: Hope for the Future* (Paulist Press, 1991) with Maureen Kelly. He also writes a regular column on parish liturgy for *Church* magazine.

JAMES B. DUNNING is a priest of the archdiocese of Seattle, Washington, and the founder of the North American Forum on the Catechumenate. He is the author of *New Wine, New Wineskins: Exploring the RCIA* (New York: Sadlier, 1981) and *Echoing God's Word* (Arlington VA: The North American Forum on the Catechumenate, 1993; available from Liturgy Training Publications).

GAEL GENSLER, OSF is pastoral minister at the Church of the Magdalene in Wichita, Kansas. She has been active in religious education and Christian initiation in several parishes, and she has been a staff member of the North American Forum on the Catechumenate.

JEANETTE MARIE LUCINIO, SP is associate professor of religious education at Catholic Theological Union, Chicago, and director of the master of arts in pastoral studies degree. She has taught in parochial schools and served as pastoral associate and parish director of religious education. For 18 years she has served as a consultant for William H. Sadlier, Inc., and has contributed to several of their catechetical publications.

JAMES W. MOUDRY is executive director and cofounder (with Christiane Brusselmans) of the Institute for the Christian Initiation of Children and a consultant for liturgy and sacramental practice. He taught theology and liturgy for 25 years at St. Paul Seminary School of Divinity of the University of St. Thomas in St. Paul, Minnesota.

RICHARD P. MOUDRY is a priest of the archdiocese of St. Paul and Minneapolis, where he served in pastoral ministry for many years, most recently as pastor of the Church of Christ the King in Minneapolis. Although officially retired, he continues to write and speak on the topic of Christian initiation.

DON NEUMANN is a priest of the diocese of Galveston-Houston. He has served as pastor, most recently at St. Pius v parish in Pasadena, Texas. He currently serves as a hospital chaplain and continues to write and speak on Christian initiation.

RICHELLE PEARL-KOLLER is a pastoral associate at the Church of Christ the King in Minneapolis, Minnesota. She is a frequent speaker and writer on the initiation of children.

STEVEN M. ROBICH was a priest of the diocese of Sioux City, Iowa. Before studying for the priesthood at St. Paul Seminary in St. Paul, Minnesota, he taught primary school for ten years and earned a graduate degree in education administration. Steven Robich died in 1992.

FRANK C. SOKOL was a priest of the diocese of Pittsburgh, Pennsylvania. He served in parish ministry and as the director of religious education/CCD in the diocese. A frequent speaker and writer on issues of Christian initiation, he served as a member of the steering committee of the North American Forum on the Catechumenate. Frank Sokol died in 1992.

VICTORIA M. TUFANO is the editor of *Catechumenate: A Journal of Christian Initiation* and other publications at Liturgy Training Publications in Chicago.

Index

All subject entries imply a relationship to the Christian initiation of children.

Acceptance, rite of, 14, 68, 99, 159

Adults, initiation of. *See* Rite of Christian Initiation of Adults (RCIA)

Age of reason. *See* Catechetical age

Alternative Futures for Worship, 6

Apostolic Tradition (Saint Hippolytus), 155

Augustine, Saint, 21

Baptism, sacrament of, 29
 of infants, ix, 14–15, 16–17, 19–20, 38–41, 54
 separation from confirmation and eucharist, 7–8
 See also Sequence of sacraments

Belloc, Hilaire, 6

Berger, Peter L., 167

Bishops, role of, 7, 8, 42, 46, 49, 55, 96

Blondel, Maurice, 166

Brusselmans, Christiane, xi, 27–28

Bultmann, Rudolf, 115

Catechesis, 8, 31–32, 39, 77–79, 107, 149–50, 167–70
 lectionary-based, x–xi, 16, 114–15, 159, 167
 modifying the cognitive character of, 9–11, 136–37
 and religious education, 9–10, 48, 50–51, 67, 93, 97, 99, 107, 109, 111–15
 twentieth-century movements in, 165–67
 See also Catechumenate

Catechesis in Our Time (Synod of Bishops), x, 77

Catechetical age, defined, 8, 52–53, 68, 71, 94, 106, 112, 135–36, 154

Catechumenate
 compared to classroom method of preparation, 111–15
 ministry teams, 88–90
 periods of, 15–16, 68–70, 98–102
 See also Catechesis

Cavalletti, Sofia, 136, 137–38, 140

"Christian Initiation of Children Who Have Reached Catechetical Age," 59–65, 67, 94, 105–6, 149
 implementation of, 173–75
 initial reaction to, viii–ix
 sample plans for implementing, 47–50, 98–102
 and unbaptized children, ix, 28, 60–61, 63, 67, 68, 80n, 85–90, 93–94
 See also Sequence of sacraments

Code of Canon Law, 28, 37, 40, 71, 76–77

Community, role of, 11–13, 14–15, 24n–25n, 29–30, 32–33, 51, 52, 63, 70–73

Companions, role of, 61–63, 69–71, 74–75, 95, 99, 108

Confession. *See* Reconciliation, sacrament of

Confirmation, sacrament of
 in sequence of sacraments, ix, 7–9, 18–19, 41–42, 46, 53, 75–77
 sponsors of, 125–29
 See also Sequence of sacraments

Constitution on the Sacred Liturgy, 13

Conversion, aspects of, 94–95, 153–60, 166, 169–70

Coudreau, Francois, 27, 35–36

Council of Trent, 7–8

Counter-Reformation, 48

Cyprian, Saint, 7

Directory for Masses with Children, xi, 63

Duffy, Regis, 29, 153

Easter Vigil, liturgy of, 23n–24n, 70, 75, 90, 95–96, 100–101

Election and enrollment of names, rite of, 63, 64, 69, 73, 81n, 100

Eucharist, sacrament of, 12–13
 catechumenal model of, 42–43
 separation from baptism and confirmation, 7–8
 See also Sequence of sacraments

Families, role of. *See* Parents and families, role of

"Family Perspective in Church and Society, A" (USCC), 31

First communion. *See* Eucharist, sacrament of

Forum. *See* North American Forum on the Catechumenate

Fowler, Jim, 15

Friedman, Edwin, 31

Fuller, Buckminster, 13

Godparents, role of. *See* Sponsors and godparents, role of

Grandparents, role of. *See* Parents and families, role of

Greeley, Andrew, 32

Griffin, Bertram, 40

179

Hippolytus, Saint, 155
Hoge, Dean, 15–16
Holeton, David, 11–12
Hovda, Robert, 30
Infants, initiation of, ix, 14–15, 16–17, 19–20, 38–41, 54
Instruction on Infant Baptism, 38–39
International Committee on English in the Liturgy (ICEL), xi, 80n
Jesus
  attitude of toward children, 10, 21, 30, 90
  as sacrament, 12–13, 17, 23n, 29
Jungmann, Josef, 114
Kavanagh, Aidan, 7, 13–14, 18, 36, 170
Keen, Sam, 17–18
Keillor, Garrison, 5, 11
Lent, as period of preparation, 63, 75, 96–97, 100
Liturgy, celebration of, 16, 52, 139, 168
Luckmann, Thomas, 167
Made Not Born (Kavanagh), 36
McKenzie, Terri, 41
Montessori, Maria, 20
Moudry, Richard, 42
Mystagogy, period of, 11, 14, 70, 101–2
National Association of Catholic Diocesan Family Life Ministers, 31
National Catechetical Directory, x, 37–38, 77
National Conference of Catholic Bishops (NCCB), 53, 55, 64, 76, 80n, 172

National Statutes on the Catechumenate, 76, 77, 101, 149
North American Forum on the Catechumenate, 27, 28
On Becoming a Catholic (Duffy), 153
Ordo Initiationis Christianae Adultorum, viii
Parents and families, role of, 14–15, 17–18, 20–21, 30–33, 38–39, 49–50, 60, 62, 68, 72–73, 85–87, 89, 98–102, 106–8, 128–29, 136–37, 145–50, 173–75
Parish, role of. *See* Community, role of
Peers, role of. *See* Companions, role of
Penance. *See* Reconciliation, sacrament of
Percy, Walker, 32–33
Pius X, 8, 48
Piviteau, Didier, 9–10
Precatechumenate, period of, 68, 80n–81n, 98–99
Purification and enlightenment, 70, 81n, 100
Quam Singulari (Pius X), 8
RCIA. *See Rite of Christian Initiation of Adults* (RCIA)
RCIC. *See* "Christian Initiation of Children Who Have Reached Catechetical Age"; *Rite of Christian Initiation of Adults* (RCIA)
Reconciliation, sacrament of, 20, 148–49
  and rite of scrutiny, 52, 69–70, 74–75, 81n, 117–22
Reformation, effects of, 48
Religious education. *See* Catechesis

Religious Potential of the Child, The (Cavalletti), 136
Rite of Baptism for Children, 73
Rite of Christian Initiation of Adults (RCIA), 5–6, 54, 80n, 93–94, 125
  implementation of, 173–75
  implications for initiation of children, 13–20, 36–43, 46–47, 73–75, 87–88
  initial reaction to, viii–ix, 28, 45–46
  and sequence of sacraments. *See* Sequence of sacraments
  See also "Christian Initiation of Children Who Have Reached Catechetical Age"
Rite of Confirmation, 18, 71, 76–77, 125–29
Rites of initiation. *See* individual rites and sacraments by name
Roberto, John, 9
Sacraments. *See* individual sacraments by name
Savelsky, Michael, 41
Scrutiny, rite of, 52, 69–70, 74–75, 81n, 117–22
Searle, Mark, 18–19, 159
Second Coming, The (Percy), 32–33
Second Vatican Council. *See* Vatican II
Segundo, Juan, 13
Sequence of sacraments, x, 6, 7–8, 10–11, 18–20, 25n, 36–38, 41–42, 46–55, 70, 75–77, 96, 128–29, 149
Sharing the Light of Faith. See National Catechetical Directory
Shea, John, 12

180

Social Construction of Reality, The (Berger & Luckmann), 167

Sokol, Frank, 28

Sponsors and godparents, role of, 15, 40–41, 43, 62, 68–70, 72–73, 106–7, 125–29, 156, 161n

Sutcliffe, John, 10–11

Symbols, importance of, 11, 32, 78, 138–41, 159, 168–69

Tertullian, 154–55

Thompson, Francis, 21

Time frame for initiation process, 39, 43, 68, 90, 95–98, 99–100, 108

Unbaptized children, ix, 28, 60–61, 63, 67, 68, 80n, 85–90, 93–94

United States Catholic Conference (USCC), 80n, 172

Vatican II, reforms of, 29, 42, 47, 49, 54, 128–29

Westerhoff, John, 136